FEARLESS

How to Avoid
Self-Sabotage and
Become a Successful Start-up
Entrepreneur

Wendy L. Elliott, MBA/HCM
Jessica L Vera Ph.D.

<u>*Copyright*</u>

regarded as affecting the validity of any trademark or service mark.

Warning and Disclaimer

As a seasoned entrepreneur and successful business owner, it's easy to think you have learned the lessons and walked the walk. But like locksmiths, Dr. Jessica Vera and Wendy Elliott opened doors in my mind to reveal fresh, new ideas and perspectives, reminding me that there is always so much more to know! More importantly, they helped me remember what it was like to find a passion and start a new venture so that I am better prepared to mentor others who are ready to launch. **FEARLESS** *takes you through an encouraging journey. Interweaving their deeply personal stories with the lives of movie characters is their effective way to provoke the reader's self-thought, as opposed to publishing a "how to" book. Bravo ladies...job well done!*

Jolanda N. Janszewski, Ph.D., MPH

CSS, Inc.

Chairman of the Board

Dr. Jessica Vera and Wendy Elliott are two ladies, who exemplify how women today are gaining recognition, how courage despite fear can positively affect women in partnership, and how collaboratively we can accomplish a great deal more, than by standing alone. In their book, FEARLESS, Dr. Jessica Vera and Wendy Elliott show us that by working together through strength, despite all past trauma and potentially negative experiences, women compliment men. The authors vulnerably put themselves out there, they inform us, educate us and inspire us. These women have "guts", they lovingly but strongly believe that we as women can and will make it, with their conviction to help others in need. This book shines with great simplicity, wisdom, and clarity, it opens your eyes to the world we live in and the greater possibilities available to us now.

Dr. Jessica Vera and Wendy Elliott have influenced my learning and have motivated me to take a new path in life. Dr. Jessica Vera illuminated me, my beliefs and capabilities. She taught me to cultivate and develop a new lifestyle; one that is intentional and geared towards deep personal fulfillment, as well as community growth. By empowering women, they both are teaching others and me how we as women can help ourselves by making small changes that can influence others on a global scale. FEARLESS is a must read for anyone desiring to find their unique something that they can offer the world, and who need the roadmap, to get into the marketplace of online entrepreneurialism.

Viviana Malamud
B.A., RHN, C.R.C., R.R.P.
CEO/Owner
Daniel´s Apart Hotel
Lima, Peru

FEARLESS is a motivating account of two women who have not only survived domestic violence and cultural inequities, but who thrived despite the challenges they faced early in life. Wendy and Jessica share deeply personal experiences that help readers trust that conquering one's fears is a matter of perception and execution. FEARLESS does a wonderful job of explaining the science behind gender roles, and the history of gender evolution. I thoroughly enjoyed this book from beginning to end.

Dennis Lauchner
Chief Executive Officer, CSS, Inc.

From Fear to Victory

From neuroscience to an historical perspective of women in the workforce, Jessica and Wendy have clearly walked their talk. Their transparency about the ups and downs of their individual life journeys gives them the authority to speak about being "Fearless" and living life with purpose with passion. We all have fears. The authors show us how to develop the courage to walk through it to victory. Thank you, Wendy and Jessica!

PPollock on April 9, 2017

Relevant, applicable and so necessary! Wendy and Jessica show readers how to focus on themselves and reach inside to tackle what is holding them back! Many books attempt to offer a new lease on life-FEARLESS delivers! This is a great group learning and revitalization workbook also. Bravo ladies! Author S.G. Savage

S.G. Savage on April 10, 2017

The advice you need to excel.

What a fitting book for this time in our life. This is an excellent revelation on how to function for excellence. Self-Sabotage is so prevalent today and this writing will reveal it and help you explode it. A must read and apply to your life.

Larry Raad April 9, 2017

Fearless

Just got into the book, with great expectations when two women collaborate, writing on such important subjects! This is one book I want to delve into wholeheartedly.

Amazon Customer on April 9, 2017

Changing Role of Women

Interesting read, even for a man. The authors write about the changing roles of women in society, and how they create opportunities for women today.

New Jersey62 on April 11, 2017

It is a great read.

This book is groundbreaking. Dealing with a number one obstacle in life. Fear. It is a great read.

Very useful information for anyone struggling with self-doubt, self-esteem, or life issues in general. Or for those who just want to learn the essence of being an entrepreneur.

5.0 out of 5 stars OUTSTANDING message for all of us!

OUTSTANDING Message for all of us!!

Jump in. Dive Deep. Find your fearless. A MUST read for women and men!

Gayle Cassidy, April 9, 2017

5.0 out of 5 starsEvery woman needs to know how to walk in fearlessness ...

Every woman needs to know how to walk in fearlessness. This book will help you to understand and walk in this.

5.0 out of 5 starsFrom Fearful to FEARLESS

5.0 out of 5 stars Five Stars

Mary Ann Seymour, April 9, 2017

Five Stars!!

Outstanding!

5.0 out of 5 starsI love that the proceeds are going to a very very ...

Dawn Huth, April 8, 2017

I love that the proceeds are going to a very very.....

Expect to be encouraged and tooled up to be a real deal woman. Wendy and Jessica are a living testament to what they write. They encourage people every week of their lives. I love that the proceeds are going to a very very worthy cause. We all need help in how to kill those giants in our lives. This book does that and more.

Anonymous

From Fearful to Fearless

Fearless is a timeless book that ALL women can relate to. The profound come-back experiences of these two warrior women are phenomenal and inspirational. You will be encouraged, motivated and ready to keep pressing in and moving through to whatever fears and difficulties that have kept you back in your career and life choices to become FEARLESS!

Dr. Becky Slabaugh on April 9, 2017

So Glad I got it!

The teamwork of these two women has produced a thought provoking and encouraging book for any woman struggling to go forth and walk out her dreams! If you are thinking of launching out on a new adventure be sure to have this in your backpack!

Cecile Bruner on April 11, 2017

CONTENTS

DEDICATION

For our parents,

First and foremost, to our Creator,
for providing the path that we follow; and
for giving us the guidance on this journey.

Wendy, to my mother, none of this would have been possible without her strong and effortless dedication to raising a strong resilient woman. To my Daddy for always making me his "little girl."

Jessica, the only girl in the bunch of five; despite the odds, mom you taught me the value of myself, hard work, and perseverance. Thank you for being my greatest cheerleader in life. To my father our path although windy, today I know that I have your love and support, thank you.

Join the Fight to Eradicate Human Exploitation
–

50% of all author royalties are donated to non-for-profits through
EliteFundsFreedom.org

FOREWORD

In the epic blockbuster movie "Gladiator", there is one scene where Maximus and his small ragtag band of warriors are pit against six (6), swift two-horse-drawn battle carriages with sharpshooter-archers who can fire arrows and long spears at will, and carriage drivers who can maneuver these war vehicles with wheels wrought with two-feet-long, sharp 'spearlets' at their spokes, so sharp they can cut through a person kneeling or sitting on the ground.

Maximus and his team seem to be at an overwhelming disadvantage, especially since they are on foot, they have no archers…and all they have are their shields and spears.

What the audience including the emperor at the Colosseum doesn't know, is that Maximums is a former Roman general who has won many battles and is a master at commanding Roman armies to strategically defeat the enemy, even if the odds are stacked against them.

While the announcer shouts the scene that they are portraying, Maximus asks, "Anyone here been in the army?" A few say they have. He replies, "You can help me. Whatever comes through these gates, we have a better chance of survival if we work together. Do you understand? If we stay together, we survive."

When the archers unleash their deadly arrows and spears, a handful of Maximus' warriors who choose to stay **isolated** from the group are instantly hit and killed.

Immediately, Maximus orders, "Come together! Come together!"

The remaining warriors come together, **lock shields** and form an impenetrable shield, like that of a turtle shell. This way, no matter which angle the archers unleash their deadly arrows, they only hit the shields.

He then shouts, "Hold! Hold!"

This means that the locked shields are held in turtle-shell formation at ground level, until Maximus roars, "Diamond! Diamond! **As one**!!"

At this command, the shields are formed into an ascending ramp, which topples one of the war carriages over.

Now let's put this story on hold and I'll come back to it in a few moments.

Dear Reader, you hold in your hands Dr. Jessica Vera and Wendy Elliott's book "Fearless", who both understand the overwhelming disadvantage of **isolating** oneself, as you go through the journey from wherever you are, to becoming a successful, fearless entrepreneur and the game-changing value of "**locking shields**".

You will deeply appreciate how both authors first establish a refreshing scientific foundation from which they build their thesis of true transformation.

What a stark contrast to several recent books I've read on entrepreneurship, that recommend change from a purely experiential basis (solely based on the author's personal experiences), and a few testimonials here and there to back their claims.

In this book, the scientific foundation, complemented with a wealth of research and statistics, firmly establish these authors' credibility, and will eliminate any doubt about the validity of each chapter.

You will also sense the care and the passion of Dr. Jessica Vera and Wendy Elliott to help women take their places in society, whether in their families or in startups, in boardrooms, or in corporate America.

Aside from this, you will also discover that their intense passion encompasses a much larger mission, which is to **lock shields** with other entrepreneurs, companies, non-profit organizations and ministries, to fight on behalf of the millions of women and children caught in human trafficking.

Over half of the profits from each book will go directly into the fight against human trafficking, which is a worldwide issue.

Both my Author-Friends truly embody the words "Courageous, Brave and Fearless."

And it is their mission to help you also become a successful startup entrepreneur.

In this book, they don't skip steps.

After they establish the solid scientific foundation, they promptly tackle the history of women in business, the pros and cons of startup women entrepreneurs, the mindsets that have held us back, and the strengths and weaknesses of women.

You will immediately connect with both Authors as they share with vulnerability and authenticity, their own personal histories, stories of separation and trauma, their difficult challenges and struggles as entrepreneurs and as team members working in corporate America.

Then they carefully lay out their **powerful blueprint** for women from whatever walk of life, who have always wanted to start a business, to move forward in the 21ST century to become wildly successful startup entrepreneurs, as more and more online opportunities for women become available.

Ok, back to the battle in the middle of the Colosseum. After the first battle carriage is demolished and its riders vanquished, Maximus tackles each of them one after the other, such that Maximus' team goes from being on the defensive, to going on the offense.

In the end, though initially at a severe disadvantage, Maximus and his warriors are the victors!

In the same way, though you may feel that the odds are stacked against you, I believe that under the leadership, mentorship and guidance of my friends and sisters-in-arms Dr. Jessica Vera and Wendy Elliott, you can go from not knowing where to start, to conquering self-limiting mindsets, then beginning your journey towards successful startup entrepreneurship.

Remember, you are not alone. I invite you to **lock shields** with my Author-Friends, on your journey towards truly becoming fearless, and succeed indeed for a much larger mission – the fight against human trafficking. **As one**!

~Jackie Morey

CustomerStrategyAcademy.com

JackieMorey.com

PERSONAL NOTE

In FEARLESS the authors, two women, who have forged through life building upon what their mothers before them accomplished and taught them, sat down to discuss and to write about the changing roles of women in society. And about how these changes challenge and create opportunities for women today.

Both authors share a passion to empower and equip women through pain to freedom to flourish in entrepreneurship (whether within an organization or self-employment), as they firmly believe that we are stronger collectively.

Women are warriors and there is an immediate need to ban together against the eradication of enslavement and trafficking of women and children worldwide.

Jessica Vera is a survivor, mother, and a wife with a PhD. She lives in Florida and was born in Peru. For years, she struggled with the feeling she was not good enough and did not deserve to be happy. She lived full of fears. Then she discovered where these feelings came from and that she was not the only one who had them. She was not alone. She was not BROKEN. She now devotes her life to sharing her story with anyone needlessly suffering with these feelings. So, every morning they can wake up with peace, joy and happiness and be free from this pain. To learn more about her story of healing go to ElitePerformanceAcademy.us

Wendy Elliott is a rural-raised, survivor of domestic violence, partner, and godmother with an MBA in Healthcare Management. She was born in West Virginia, and now lives in Florida. She was raised by her grandparents who adopted her at an early age. She has struggled for years with the fears of not being good enough, failure and letting her grandparents' down. An inspired overachiever, Wendy has worked in the corporate arena for most of her adult career holding various leadership positions. But with the turning tides in healthcare, Wendy has learned firsthand of the pain of loss and the insecurity caused by a lack of control over one's employment stability within the corporate culture. To learn more about her story of healing go to EltePerformanceAcademy.us

The combined experiences and expertise of these 'YaYa' sisters bring to life on each page of this book what it means to be a multifaceted unique woman within the context of a collective consciousness of humanity in the 21st century age of technology.

They provide clear and concise informed content about where women historically have been socialized to be, the impact of economic trends in the US and globally on gender roles, and provide insight on how women can take a seat at their table, if they so desire.

Today in the United States and in the developing world, women are better off than ever.

We stand on the shoulders of the women who came before us, women who had to fight for the rights that we take for granted and do not always exercise.

One truth remains though; men still govern most of the countries in the world. Of the 195 independent countries, only 17 are led by women.

Even though women are over 50 percent of the college graduates and make up of overall population in the United States, the percentage of women entrepreneurs (only 5%), in corporate and board leadership and elected congressional officials is not comparable with our gender counterpart.

Proportion of seats held by women in national parliament in 2014, was 19.4% (genderstats.un.org)

Leveling the gender disparity on the playground, is now possible, when assets, resources, and innovation are leveraged to deconstruct beliefs about leadership, work, love, and play.

FEARLESS

Introduction

What would you do if you were not fearful?

This book was written for women of today and tomorrow, as well as for exceptionally evolved men, who identify with their fear, but despite them have an adventurous and inquisitive mind. It is for all who are seeking to learn from their experience in order to release abundant potential inherently and uniquely theirs to heal and experience freedom to flourish.

The authors are members of a socially-responsible community that is made up of individuals, who are enmeshed by shared life experiences, commitment to life learning and to the reengineering of the socially constructed meaning of success, to change the world, one soul at a time, for the good of all humanity.

Each member comes from a different walk through life, but intentional meaningfulness is immeasurably valued and respected. An upheld belief that is supported by the law of economics and many studies of diversity is that if we tap into the entire pool of human resources and talents, our collective performance will improve.

Therefore, if you are reading this book, then know that if you will take a risk on yourself then you will experience life as you have always desired. And the achievements will extend beyond mere individual to collective benefit for us all.

However, this book is not for you, if you view this four-letter word as vulgar--WORK. Because there is work in refinement and in the development of something wonderfully unique and valuable for you and others.

Read on, if you desire to tap into your essence as a woman, fuel your passions, and want to learn to leverage your unique assets to go from a day job to your dream life. In the following pages, we will deconstruct and reengineer many of socialized beliefs that we in the Western world (particularly) have cultivated about gender roles and that perpetuate stagnation and precipitate many of our shared fears. The fear of not being enough, valued, loved, of being a failure and so on...

To clarify our intent in writing FEARLESS, is not to dispel that fear is real, but rather to empower and to equip you, the reader, to recognize that fear is an emotion embedded in beliefs that can be overridden, to take meaningful action, despite them.

Know that you are not alone. Many fears are shared and experienced by everyone, an examination from a scientific perspective offered by George L. Lindenfeld, Ph.D. (clinical psychologist), eloquently explains that at the core belief about fears, particular to trauma or a perceived traumatic experience is the fact that it's not the trauma itself that is lasting, but rather the fear memories that cannot be forgotten.

For example, an impressionable traumatic/loss experience using scientific methodologies such as EEG data (Thatcher Life Span Reference Data Base, Evenas & Abarbanel, 1999) can provide visual demonstrations of what happens to the brain when a traumatic memory resurfaces. The brain lights up (brain on fire) in such a way that re-experiencing occurs.

Dr. Agren explained in his 2012 Uppsala dissertation (Koffman, 2012) that fear memories are made stable and permanent through a process called consolidation that stretches on for hours after the initial encoding. And that when the fear memories are recalled, it is restored in the brain through a process called reconsolidation.

Based upon these and many other scientific findings there is a great deal of work being done in the arena of memory research with promising outcomes for individuals, who suffer from severe stress and anxiety (post-traumatic stress disorder and related symptomatology).

Did you know for example that our minds and bodies harbor memories from experiences? They do, and it is because of this phenomenon that it is very helpful to be aware of your senses in situations. Drop in to how the situation makes you feel. Then respond rather than react. Taking account in the present that what you are feeling is what you are feeling and it is not absolute truth. All too often we create conditions that promote fear reactions. Depending upon your past experiences knowing that you are feeling fear, is your mind and body's way of alerting a response. Utilize this emotional information to your advantage, by testing the reality of the situation, and then act in a manner that promotes you and those around you.

Remember fear emits a vibration that is negative and attracts more of the same. However, you can assume control over your emotions with practice.

We want to share with you that our shared fear in writing this book was that we could not get it done. Collaborative writing is one of the hardest tasks to accomplish, because it means meshing ideas, beliefs, experiences, and knowledge from two different perspectives in a manner that appears seamless. Tack on the varied demands on each author's life and you have an equation with a possible negative outcome. Thank God for skilled editors.

SCENE I

NOW here we go. Come to the edge. We might fall.
Come to the edge. It's too high!
COME TO THE EDGE!
And they came, and He pushed, and they flew.

-Christopher Log

CHAPTER1: The Devil Wears Prada or Just the Overachievers?

If you are not getting the results you'd like or need from any activity, situation, or relationship, it's probably because your goals are not clearly enough defined, to yourself and to others.
– Paul J. Meyer

When a woman is in a leadership role, she is perceived by her peers as a tyrant or masculine, due to exhibiting the very behaviors that are all too often expected of men in the same position.

But is this truth or perception based upon a historical lens influenced by the socialization of women in the western world and beyond?

Do women have to undertake male characteristics to be perceived as competent in the workforce?

Do you think of her as fearless?

Let's start the conversation by exploring current trends. Hollywood plays an instrumental part in providing pictorial representations of our social constructs of the role of women today. In fact, sociologist suggest that pop culture is a reflection of what we truly believe. (Livesey, Chris, AS Sociology for AQA. 2nd ed. UK:Hodder Education, 2005).

In this oldie but goodie motion picture. The Devil Wears Prada, do you remember it? The stage is set, Meryl Streep's character is the head of a large fashion icon magazine. She is portrayed as a ruthless, ambitious, and conniving business woman, with a killer wardrobe and an affluent envied lifestyle.

Enter the protagonist, a young aspiring writer, who quickly learns the rules of the game. She finds herself transforming into a version of her boss, in order to excel and receive praise and acceptance by Meryl's character and others at work. The interesting aspect of the movie, beyond the beautiful location shots, killer wardrobe and the attractive male supporting role, is the epiphany had by the protégé that she must lose herself, her identity as an "integrious' aspiring writer, her boyfriend of years, and her close friends, in order to be in, the "in" and valued.

After a short period of being among those she so aspired to be like, she realizes that she would rather lose access to Prada, than herself. She quits her dream job, to pursue her passion and reconnects with her former self, although a little wiser and more confident, she now presumably knows what she does not want to become.

Meryl's character although successful by outside measures, was on her third divorce, her children were being raised by others with a portrayed attitude of entitlement and privilege, and it is communicated that she made choices along her career path that led to the experience of all those loses in favor of maintaining her power position, status, and access to wear Prada whenever she pleased.

Two very different women, but several similar themes arise in the movie.

Women need to feel valued in what they do. Whether it be in leadership, as a mom, wife, or entrepreneur. When that sense of value or worth as defined by the outside and then internalized is lacking it can have devastating impact on self-esteem and potential.

The other principle emerging theme, as it pertains to the modern world of work as tackled in the movie, is that as more women enter or re-enter the workforce, seeking to achieve leadership in established organizations or to maintain integrity in their work, they are faced with the conundrum that in order to achieve success choices have to be intentionally made. Why you might be asking yourself? Because the world of work and support systems of finance remain predominantly male domains.

A Valued Woman is a Fulfilled Woman

Let's tackle the first theme, why do women have the need to be valued by others?

And how is this impacting the role of women in the workforce and beyond?

To answer these foundational questions in keeping with the topic of this book, how to navigate through our fears to avoid self-sabotage and become successful in entrepreneurship, as only women can, to flourish, we explored gender differences and their impact on vocational potential.

Most studies indicate that unlike men, who were socialized (in most cultures) to be competitive since childhood, women traditionally were socialized to be complacent, submissive, humble, and proper & pretty, due to their expected gender roles as nurturers, caretakers, wives, mothers and keepers of the home, as our principle domain.

That is why, when we encounter our sisters in the work place, who are competitive, it takes us aback at times. It is sometimes misinterpreted as emulating one of the boys, in order to play on the playground. And it very well may be. More on this in a bit.

An examination of the historical origins of the role of women may assist us in understanding where our need for value originates.

If we go back to the story of creation in the longest running number one best seller book in the world, the Bible. We learn in Genesis 1 and 2 that Adam, although created first and having dominion over all the animals, was alone and isolated because none of the animals of creation could relate to him. It was not until God created women from Adam's rib that a counterpart was born.

There are many commentaries on the bible and most conclude that women are image bearers of God, just like men. We were created as co-workers who share authority and responsibility for multiplying and governing the earth. Women are equal, but different, and prepared to come alongside and aid others. This is Wendy and Jessica's shared view point.

However, we were not created the same as man. Rather, complimentary to the innate characteristics of man.

The Role of Women - Nature versus Nurture

What we know about the Biochemistry of Women (Nature):

Both Wendy and Jessica share a love for science. Therefore, we are going to summarize what is found in the scientific literature to explain gender differences. In particular, as found in the field of neuroscience.

Neuroscience is a relatively young discipline. Therefore, although there is increasing research being completed, please read the following with a critical mind. Research is infinitely powerful, when there is consensus about the findings, but this does not happen typically. Hence why it is that the world of scientific research is unending and forever evolving.

The very reason for research is to explore possibilities, but a factor to consider is that the direction of research all too often is influenced by systemic cultural economic trends. Therefore, you will find that we will use language such as 'generally speaking' or 'in most cases' to qualify our research findings on gender differences.

For the purposes of this book, we chose to focus on the following, which have been identified in many literature and books reviewed, as compared to our male counterparts, women are better at;

(a) Communication, specifically verbal fluency,

(b) Integrating intuition and reasoning,

(c) Emotional intelligence (integrating nonverbal cues, experience [memories] and related emotions),

(d) Building community through nurturing relationship; and

(e) Switch-tasking (women are masters).

Are boys and girls brains different?

Basics about Human Brain Anatomy

The human brain is the command center for the human nervous system. It receives input from the sensory organs and sends output to the muscles. It weighs about 3.3 lbs. (1.5 kilograms). The brain makes up about 2 percent of a human's body weight. The cerebrum makes up 85 percent of the brain's weight. It contains about 86 billion nerve cells (neurons) — the "gray matter". It contains billions of nerve fibers (axons and dendrites) — the "white matter". These neurons are connected by trillions of connections, or synapses.

The largest part of the human brain is the cerebrum, which is divided into two hemispheres. Underneath lies the brainstem, and behind that sits the cerebellum. The outermost layer of the cerebrum is the cerebral cortex, which consists of four lobes: the frontal lobe, the parietal lobe, the temporal lobe and the occipital lobe.

Like all vertebrate brains, the human brain develops from three sections known as the forebrain, midbrain and hindbrain. Each of these contains fluid-filled cavities called ventricles. The forebrain develops into the cerebrum and underlying structures; the midbrain becomes part of the brainstem; and the hindbrain gives rise to regions of the brainstem and the cerebellum.

The cerebral cortex is greatly enlarged in human brains, and is considered the seat of complex thought. Visual processing takes place in the occipital lobe, near the back of the skull. The temporal lobe processes sound and language, and includes the hippocampus and amygdala, which play roles in memory and emotion, respectively. The parietal lobe integrates input from different senses and is important for spatial orientation and navigation.

The brainstem connects to the spinal cord and consists of the medulla oblongata, pons and midbrain. The primary functions of the brainstem include: relaying information between the brain and the body; supplying some of the cranial nerves to the face and head; and performing critical functions in controlling the heart, breathing and consciousness.

Between the cerebrum and brainstem lie the thalamus and hypothalamus. The thalamus relays sensory and motor signals to the cortex and is involved in regulating consciousness, sleep and alertness. The hypothalamus connects the nervous system to the endocrine system— where hormones are produced — via the pituitary gland.

The cerebellum lies beneath the cerebrum and has important functions in motor control. It plays a role in coordination and balance, and may also have some cognitive functions. Whoa, glad that mini science lesson is over.

For our purposes this information was necessary to ensure that when discussing research findings, we all understand how the brain function is different between the genders.

Women were born to talk...

There is no mistaking when two or more women get together for a girls' night, the main entertainment is conversation. We can talk for hours on the same topic or take a trip through topics of interest with ease and comfort. We love to share with our girlfriends.

One of the principle complaints heard in couple's counseling by Jessica is that women do not feel heard by their partners, because men are less inclined to engage in hours on end of discussion. They want to get to the point, just the facts.

It is a known fact that girls learn language faster than boys. Researchers for years have agreed that boys' and girls' brains are differently activated in the function of language. In a study completed by researchers from Northwestern University and the University of Haifa it was demonstrated both that areas of the brain associated with language work harder in girls than in boys during language tasks, and that boys and girls rely on different parts of the brain when performing these tasks.

Specifically, study results suggested that language processing is more sensory in boys and more abstract in girls, also that girls showed significantly greater activation in language areas of the brain than boys.

This could explain why women often provide more context and abstract representation than men. Ask a woman for directions and you may hear something like: "Turn left on Main Street, go one block past the drug store, and then turn right, where there's a flower shop on one corner and a cafe across the street."

Such information-laden directions may be helpful for women because all information is relevant to the abstract concept of where to turn; however, men may require only one cue and be distracted by additional information.

There is surmounting literature of gender difference in verbal fluency. Specifically, a study completed by Burton, Henninger and Hafetz 2010 found that a study of 134 university students, utilizing the Thurstone Word Fluency Test, revealed that women have better verbal expressive communication skills, when compared to their male counterparts. The study population being university studies, supports the belief that although some studies have demonstrated that the gap between genders lessens with maturity, women still maintain their edge in verbal fluency well into adulthood.

Also, as our brains have two hemispheres, we women use both sides of the brain when processing information; whereas men only use the left side of the brain. A similar pattern of brain processing occurs when it comes to listening

Dr. Michael Phillips, a neuro-audiologist at the Indiana University School of Medicine, found that in men only the left hemisphere is active while listening, while both hemispheres are activated in women. That is why it has been suggested that when men process language they use more sensory information such as visual and oral cues; while women use the language center of the brain to process information more holistically.

A man's ability to process language through sensory associations may help him quickly identify sights and sounds that are associated with danger, which is great to act to protect. But as women we process information differently this may account for the reason our pattern of communication is more cyclical and emotionally-laden, providing context, and intrinsic details.

The latter mode of communication is not always well appreciated by our counterparts, particularly in a corporate setting, but it lends itself well to higher intellectual reasoning, problem solving and establishment of trusting relationship. Cold facts, which is the preferred mode of information communication of males, does not always tell the entire story.

We are emotionally intelligent, intuitive beings...

Women use of both sides of our brain to help draw conclusions, because we use both intuition and analysis, rather than just numbers. In men's brains, the neuronal connectivity runs from the front of the brain to the back of each hemisphere, not across both hemispheres like a woman's. The front of a man's brain processes a problem and immediately sends information to the back of the brain, which coordinates action.

Here again lies an inherit difference, whereas men typically want to take action to solve a problem, women want to think about it. In essence, women want to integrate all the information and discuss it with others to have a sounding board.

Intuition also seems to be one of our gifts, because the part of the brain which helps with social awareness and interpersonal judgment is larger in women than in men, which may in part account for this.

Another region of the brain that is larger in women than man is the limbic system, which is the seat of emotions and memories. Embedded within the limbic system are structures that work together to store away emotional memories. These structures are not just larger in comparison to the same structures of men's brains, but we also process emotional memories on both sides of our brain. This may account for why it is that women seem to process, express, and retrieve emotions faster.

Blend all these findings and it is easier to understand why women find the expression and analysis of emotions are part of the problem-solving process. In contrast men tend to use the left side of their brains for language and the right side to process emotions. This makes it less likely that a man will express his feelings verbally. When it comes to expressing and responding to emotions, men and women are often at the opposite ends of the spectrum.

Women intentionally engage to build relationships

Staying on the thread of science, there is a hormone called oxytocin, which acts as an anti-stress hormone that decreases anxiety and fearfulness and increases relaxation. Women produce more of this estrogen-driven hormone than men do. We also have a greater capacity for empathy and due to our ability to express emotions we have a need to not only befriend other women but to form alliances. Coming together helps us comfort one another, contributes to safety, and accelerates completing critical tasks.

Are we really master multitaskers?

Let's clear up the vernacular misnomer. The brain is not designed to do a number of things at one time, especially if language is involved. What is a more accurate description is expeditious task switching.

Women have the advantage over men when it comes to task switching in part due to socialization, as women we are expected to have the capability to do multiple things at once. However, investigators are trying to determine if multitasking is a part of a women's biological make-up. One reason we have a greater affinity and proficiency for it is because we use both hemispheres of our brain giving us a greater capacity to juggle multiple activities.

Another explanation posited that during pregnancy, birth, and lactation, the hormonal fluctuation may rewire areas of the brain, which improves a woman's ability to multitask. This skill set, which some argue are innately accessible to women, when cultivated and positioned appropriately led to enhanced self-efficacy and relationship building to promote trust in community (including the workplace).

However, predominant feminine skills are not yet fully valued as parallel to competitiveness and its counterpart ambition which are synonymous with success in a still predominately male driven workforce.

In modern western culture, emotional intelligence is often devalued in the work place and an exponentially greater value on task achievement and outcomes remains the norm; without much concern for the feelings and the impact of associated behaviors on others. Therefore, task switching ability may not be as valued in the boardroom, as it is in the home domain, where we juggle multiple projects at once, while feeding the child in our arms, and speaking on the telephone.

What we know about the historical socialization of Women (Nurture):

As emotional beings, women have been socialized to extract our value from external perceptions from others. A historical review of the role of women may help to further explain why this may be.

In A Cultural History of Women, In Antiquity, Janet Tulloch (who edited the book) provides a fascinating cross-cultural lineage of the role of women. In Greco-Roman society from 500 B.C.E. – 1000 C.E. As you might suspect both societies were patriarchal and man determined a woman's lot. Hence females were treated as an object of commodity to be used and exchanged.

During this time, Aristotle believed that a female was a version of a deformed man. Women were thought to be lazy with excessive cravings for sex and food. Therefore, to control them, it was concluded that women should be under male guardianship, married, and contained behind a veil.

Philostratus, a Greek philosopher, proposed that women were particularly dangerous because a female had the capability of dissipating a man's vital fluid, leaving him unmanned.

Yet, in Judaism, although women once had positions of respect, due to their ability to procreate and maintain the purity of the family lineage. Various rabbinical writings in Jewish civil law (Talmud) led this respect to change based on the negative attributes assigned to women. In these writings, females are depicted as jealous, vain, gossipers, lazy and gluttonous.

Jewish women, like in other cultures of the time, were under the authority of their immediate kin or husbands. A woman's primary domain at the time was her home.

Fast forward to the turn of the 19th century during the Victorian period men and women's roles became more sharply defined than at any time in history. In earlier centuries, it had become usual for women to work alongside husbands and brothers in the family business. Living 'over the shop' made it easy for women to help by serving customers or keeping accounts while also attending to their domestic duties.

As the 19th century progressed men increasingly commuted to their place of work – the factory, shop or office. Wives, daughters and sisters were left at home all day to oversee the domestic duties that were increasingly carried out by servants.

The two sexes now inhabited what Victorians thought of as 'separate spheres', only coming together at breakfast and again at dinner.

The ideology of Separate Spheres rested on a definition of the 'natural' characteristics of women and men. Women were considered physically weaker yet morally superior to men, which meant that they were best suited to the domestic sphere.

Not only was it their job to counterbalance the moral taint of the public sphere in which their husbands labored all day, they were also preparing the next generation to carry on this way of life. The fact that women had such great influence at home was used as an argument against giving them the vote.

Women did, though, require a new kind of education to prepare them for this role of 'Angel in the House'. Rather than attracting a husband through their domestic abilities, middle-class girls were coached in what were known as 'accomplishments'. These would be learned either at boarding school or from a resident governess.

In *Pride & Prejudice* the snobbish Caroline Bingley lists the skills required by any young lady who considers herself accomplished: A woman must have a thorough knowledge of music, singing, drawing, dancing, and the modern languages….; and besides all this, she must possess a certain something in her air and manner of walking, the tone of her voice, her address and expressions…

As Miss Bingley emphasizes, it was important for a well-educated girl to soften her erudition with a graceful and feminine manner. No-one wanted to be called a 'blue-stocking', the name given to women who had devoted themselves too enthusiastically to intellectual pursuits.

Blue-stockings were considered unfeminine and off-putting in the way that they attempted to challenge men's 'natural' intellectual superiority. Some doctors reported that too much study actually had a damaging effect on the ovaries, turning attractive young women into dried-up prunes. Later in the century, when Oxford and Cambridge opened their doors to women, many families refused to let their clever daughters attend for fear that they would make themselves unmarriageable.

In the U.S. it was not until Ratified on August 18, 1920, that the 19th Amendment to the U.S. Constitution granted American women the right to vote—a right known as woman suffrage. At the time the U.S. was founded, its female citizens did not share all of the same rights as men, including the right to vote. It was not until 1848 that the movement for women's rights launched on a national level with a convention in Seneca Falls, New York, organized by abolitionists Elizabeth Cady Stanton (1815-1902) and Lucretia Mott (1793-1880). Following the convention, the demand for the vote became a centerpiece of the women's rights movement. Stanton and Mott, along with Susan B. Anthony (1820-1906) and other activists, formed organizations that raised public awareness and lobbied the government to grant voting rights to women. After a 70-year battle, these groups finally emerged victorious with the passage of the 19th Amendment across all states on March 22, 1984.

Interestingly that midst, by the mid-19th century, American women found themselves playing an important role during the WWII, both at home and in uniform. In 1939, the United States committed itself to total war after the Japanese attacked Pearl Harbor that included recruiting and employing women out of the home.

During this time, women worked in defense plants and volunteered for war-related organizations, in addition to managing their households. When men left for combat, women became streetcar 'conductorettes', proficient cooks, housekeepers, managed finances, fixed the car, worked, and wrote letters to their solider husbands.

Nearly 350,000 American women served in uniform, both at home and abroad volunteering for newly formed Women's Army Corps, the Navy Women's Reserve, Marine Corps Women's Reserve, Coast Guard Women's Reserve and Women's Airforce Service Pilots and the Army and Navy Nurses Corps.

At the end of the war, even though women surveyed wanted to keep their jobs, many were forced out by the men returning from the war and due to the turndown demand for war materials. Women veterans also encountered roadblocks when they tried to take advantage of benefit programs for veterans like the G.I. Bill. The nation that needed their help in a time of crisis, it seems, was not yet ready for the greater social equality that would slowly come in the decades to follow.

Even though the role of women has evolved situationally, the percentage of women in the workforce and as owner-operators or leaders in Fortune 500 companies remains incremental, when compared to our gender counterparts.

In the U.S., the Equal Pay Act of 1963 was to have leveled the remuneration gap between men and women in the workforce. On the surface, it is an illegal practice to discriminate pay based upon gender. However, in reality, we as women have yet to achieve equality of pay for work comparable to men.

These undertones have led to the increasing rise of women's movements for liberation. However, pop culture, such as the movie portrayal in the Devil Wears Prada, continue to perpetuate gender bias and stereotyping.

We are not of the belief that we are seeking to be men, or to possess the same innate characteristics and attributes as men. Rather, we need to be recognized and valued for our gender differences and what we bring to the table that is complimentary.

However, the latter has been misinterpreted even by our own gender as having to purport and advocate for oneself even to the detriment of our sisters.

20th century, Thomas Plante wrote in Psychological Today that the "all about me" battle cry is invading our culture. As a culture, our behavior is becoming more demanding, entitled, and self-centered.

If Plante's opinion is universally shared, then we as women are uniquely equipped to have a tremendous impact, as we were created to collaborate, care for one another, and to be responsible for the collective wellbeing of the generation to come.

The key for us as women is that we not forget our uniqueness, in favor of becoming one of the boys.

We have to deconstruct what is exemplified in the movie, that when a woman achieves higher education, lands a leadership position in a prominent company, or has significant success in an entrepreneurial start-up and gains visibility and so on...her behavior within this standout role is dissected and given meaning based upon luck, coincidence, must have used her feminine appeal to sleep her way up the ladder, or she had to have just duplicated others' business or was on 'the list'. This dialogue that she has adopted a male persona to maintain her power because she is part of a minority classification, so of course she had to receive preferential standing, must be socially reframed.

The worst part about this rhetoric is that the harshest critics are often found among our own sisters in business. The gossip mill initiates dialogue such as she is a ball-breaker, b.i.t.c.h., selfish, unfeeling, want-a-be-man. You get the idea.

Men typically do not waste time talking about each other, instead they challenge and stretch each other, knowing that the fastest runner will get to the finish line. And afterwards, once they lick their wounds when they have not been the winner on this occasion, you'll find them at happy-hour talking about their battle and laughing.

This type of gentlemanly jousting in the office leads to personal and company growth typically and strengthens their vocational skills for the next challenge.

In this same scenario, women in contrast ruminate, cut themselves into pieces, because "of course they did not do something right or good enough" and they are not told otherwise. Further, the failure/loss becomes an internalized value statement about their worth and competence. It serves to defeat, deplete and to demoralize.

Women often retreat into themselves and all too often they are less willing in the future to 'lean in' and to take chances. The fear of failure becomes stifling of all innate potential and it becomes a catalyst for future emotional blocks.

This brings to mind a personal example from Wendy in which while in a leadership position within a hospital system that had only promoted a few women into leadership, the latter occurred. Wendy was charged with the responsibility of taking a nonproductive division out of the red. Over the course of her employment, significant power struggles emerged among some of the old timers, who were women in mid-level leadership positions and wanted things to stay status quo. One in particular set out to undermine her efforts, as she recognized the momentum Wendy was gaining.

Wendy took the division from loss to breakeven to profitable within a year. But this did not sit well with this woman. Soon, Wendy began attending management meetings in which everything she brought forward was shut down, by the ranks. Her colleague had convinced others in management to share her negative opinions of Wendy's work. It got so bad that Wendy started to question her sanity. Because things were being said that she had no recollection of.

Wendy recalls this time vividly because it was a devastating time in her career. It was the first time that she experienced how another woman could tear her down to the point that she could no longer be effective in her job. Wendy started having panic attacks and exhibited avoidant behavior because she just did not want to face work, which was so not her.

Eventually, Wendy had no choice but to leave that position. She also made the choice to leave the organization, but really that job impacted more than just her livelihood, it took her confidence about her skills and abilities. She could not understand how one person's undermining could impact everyone's observations of her work. It would be a year before Wendy would feel sufficiently ready to take on the challenges of a new position, but the trauma that was caused, continues in some ways to haunt her even today. Every so often she is triggered, and the fear of failure, of being incompetent in the eyes of others creeps up threatening to undermine her confidence and success.

Preparing for a future not yet even in plain sight

Another fascinating experience and trend found in literature as it pertains to the role of women and work is that women are primarily socialized to prepare for the future, when the future is not even certain.

As little girls, we are still being raised by women, who teach us to dream about finding Mr. Right, having children and the perfect home but now we also hear, "Make sure you gain access to a good profession." Education has taken on a new meaning and depending upon one's family system (single parent home etc.) there may be greater importance placed on being self-sufficient economically. These predicative themes under toe the way opportunities are perceived.

If a woman is given a chance for a growth opportunity or promotion that involves a level of commitment that would interfere with her life plan that includes marriage etc., she may not even consider it because she is preoccupied with the need to be prepared for her wedding and child birthing years. Unconsciously her use of language and lack of willingness to take risks, takes her out of the running, before she's even in the race.

Or in contrast there are also women, who consciously make the decision to pursue their career, as their central identity. Therefore, relationships, children and family do not even factor into the equation. But, when a certain age is reached and they reflect upon their life, feelings of missing out, a lack of family etc. emerge.

The paradoxical conundrum that arises from these experiences is believed to be at the core of why women tend to need to be valued for what they do.

Remembering that in the past, women were valued for how well they put themselves together physically (nice dresses, make-up, but not too much, hair, nails etc.), cooked for their family, their husband's work identity, how well they kept house and their child's etiquette. All tasks that make-up one of the hardest jobs in the world, homemaker. Sally Williamson describes women in leadership still sometimes focusing on this in her book "The Hidden Factor: Executive Presence." She believes that women have the inherent ability to lead but they get in their own way of success by not using those talents effectively, by using unintentional habits that get in their way of being successful in the firm.

However, keeping in mind that historically women desiring to work outside the scope of wife and mother were criticized, ostracized, and at times told "no." A woman in the workforce, when it was not a financial household necessity, was shunned.

These historical beginnings predisposed by a women's perception of herself in the context of the era. Yet, today even though women seeking higher education and are accessing (in greater numbers) ivy-league opportunities, the stats remain staggeringly surprising that we do not hold a greater percentage of leadership roles in corporate America, global government, or academia.

Even when the world economy set the stage for the need for women to work; such as during the WWII and cyclical periods of economic depression, today although more acceptable, women are still not sitting at the same table as men, as often as they could. Or are considered in the running, never hitting the top echelon of power.

When they do sit at the same table, the paradox becomes remaining a viable opponent and asset, while juggling all the other roles chosen (daughter, wife, mother, grandmother etc.), leaving little room to mentor sisters striving for the same objectives.

The choice can result in secondary isolation from the very peers we desire to promote. Also, being perceived as a cold heartless, uncaring selfish woman, who is not at the PTA meetings with home baked goods for her kids, but rather brings or sends in store bought, and who is not able to be fully attentive to one demand for her attention at a time.

Funny enough, taking a seat at the table, has resulted in us not only failing in the very roles we had been taught to dream about, but we have yet to figure out fully, how to transfer our innate unique skills sets, into the labor market and to gain the recognition and value desired.

Just to recap, among the unique skill sets of a woman are her ability to master emotional intelligence, expressive communication, building relationships through trust, logical thinking and use of intuition, master-taskers and altruism.

The key to minimizing the impact of our confidence conundrum is to shift our mindset, recognizing that we bring uniqueness, to a male-originated work culture and to courageously take risks, despite the possibility of failure. Whether your aspiration is to be the head of a Fortune 500 company or your own company, head of state, or head of your household, value your feminine difference, embrace that we compliment men, not compete against them, and enhance those skills that will serve your desired vocational path.

Can we really have it all?

Based upon the Hollywood portrayals of powerful women in the movies, it does not appear we can. However, we are intent on offering a different perspective on this response.

As women, we are gifted with the ability of master-taskers and we are multidimensional by design. We are someone's daughter, object of affection, and some of us take on the roles of wife, mother, caretaker, coworker, colleague, boss, business woman etc.

The question is not can we really have it all. Rather, it is more accurately stated how can we have it all?

Depending upon the season you find yourself in, there are choices to be made. The first of which is taking responsibility for yourself and your choices.

For example, do I make the cookies or buy them for the mother's PTA meeting for my child's school? If I make them, it will take me a few hours of time, but I might be able to create an activity for my child and me to do together. But then again, I don't know how to bake, because my mom worked when I was a child and she never taught me. Also, if I learn to bake them, they might not turn out well and what will the other mothers' say about my kid and her mother. The same thing might occur, if I buy the cookies. I could also consider having them made for me and then I can pretend that I did the work, and no one would be the wiser.

This example might appear trivial on the surface, but the reality is that this simple scenario is what women of all walks of life are faced with at different points on a continuum of being, whether in the home, work or community. There is an exchange that has to be considered and then a choice made.

If you do this, what implications are there? And once the options are weighed out then, the choice is made. Depending upon the outcome you will either feel fabulous or beat yourself up repeatedly because of the value surrounding the experience.

It is these experiences of perceived failure that can precipitate the feeling of fear and faulty thinking, which then unfortunately either leads to doing nothing or repeating patterns of behavior to avoid pain.

In Jessica's case, although now a trauma graduate, once she was a sexually abused child, who experienced repeated exploitation early on. And because of the created vulnerabilities resulting from repeated negative experiences she learned early on about differentials in power, coercion, shame, guilt and eventually self-deprecation.

As an emerging adult, Jessica can honestly say that she operated from a position of constant fear. The core theme being that she could not ever let them know the truth about her past. Therefore, an extraverted persona was created, who everyone loved.

Achievement became the purpose of all activities, in order to gain outward recognitions, accolades, and the praises of others. But despite gaining multiple degrees, abundance of resources, position, outward recognition and the love Jessica so thought she desperately needed, the truth was that she remained empty.

There were moments in time, when Jessica thought okay, "I've made it". One particular time comes to mind. Jessica was likely 24 years old. She had just completed her initial formal studies in psychology and vocational rehabilitation. One failed marriage behind her, she was faced with the life changing experience of having the only provider and caregiver in her life, her mom, fall suddenly ill, unable to work.

Choice at the time, was not even considered. Jessica's mom was in and out of the hospital. She had a younger brother, who was still in school. They were about to lose their rental and there was nothing financially coming into the household.

Jessica went to bed that night, talked to the universe, because she did not have an intimate relationship with her Creator at that time, and said "And now what?"

Overnight she had a download that would change the trajectory of her life path. She dreamt of an organization that could help ethnic minorities regain their power position, in a system that did not foster it. The system at the time leveraged the person's ignorance of the language, legalese, and the systemic tort culture to subrogate (reallocate) liability and pay out as minimal as possible to the victim.

This left many non-Anglo ethnic people with minimal resources to access goods and services to rehabilitate themselves after an accident. To counter balance the system, she created corporations that employed professionals from different subcultural ethnic minority communities represented in Canada and provided culturally sensitive advocacy, disability management, and vocational rehabilitation services in various languages.

The success of the companies exceeded far beyond anything that she had ever imagined. The best way to describe it, was that her personal resources and those that she could access went from zero to a million overnight.

Jessica thought, this is it, success!

But when the daze of what had been accomplished and the novelty of continued growth began to wear off, Jessica's perception of the negativity around her became very vivid. Jessica was now surrounded by many people, who gave a lot of what she thought she needed, but yet she felt so alone.

Jessica had been making the choice of work over relationships for years, because she did not really believe that there existed a man in the world, who could love the real her. The one who no one had ever gotten to really know yet.

So Jessica made the choice to focus on pursuit of happiness in relationship, since the joy of abundant resources had fizzled. Not meaning for this to sound trivial, because she firmly believes that we need and want resources, but what she is trying to communicate is that resources alone cannot replace or provide love (at least that was her experience).

Also, there was another principle operating in Jessica's mind at the time. The concept of desire versus deserving. You can desire to have money, things, etc., but when you don't really believe that you deserve abundance, then you purpose to burn through it (the resources) quite effortlessly. AND believe it when Jessica says, it does not take much to burn through millions under these conditions.

The other fascinating experience was that when Jessica redirected her attention to finding value in relationships, she went from one man to another. Each person, she found met some of her needs, but none met them all.

Like most young women, Jessica had envisioned her prince charming as a little girl. He was her rescuer, protector warrior, who was beautiful, strong, but gentle. He was physical, but also an intellect and most assuredly in touch with his feminine side, because how else would they be able to talk for hours on end.

Sadly, while Jessica was out seeking, the doing in her corporations was dwindling, because her focus on work was distracted by matters of the heart. Jessica is so very grateful that she was blessed with achieving sustainability for a time.

The corporations provided an inheritance that Jessica otherwise would have never received. With the residual resources, she pursued further education (till this day), but this time without the concurrent pressure of having to work three jobs to pay for it. Jessica was also blessed with the ability to be generous.

Sometime later, Jessica would learn that she had been the focus of a great deal of ridicule within the organizations she created. Jessica had been perceived similar to that of Meryl's character in the movie. This was a difficult revelation to learn of, but now happily married, to her partner in life, for the last 20 years, and having the privilege to raise two beautiful girls, she can honestly say that she has no regrets about her decision to pursue marriage and family, at the time.

But, just like the protégé in the movie, in this season of her life, she is ready and all the conditions in her life are aligned to support a reemergence in the world of high-tech entrepreneurship.

Over the last year, Jessica has devoted herself to learning all there is to know about doing business on the internet. It is her belief that unlike any other time in history, there is an opportunity for women to gain access to online streams of income that will balance the inequality otherwise experienced in the workforce.

Wendy shares this sentiment and believes that from her perspective, women are gaining recognition in the boardroom that in the past was not customary. She shares, "Leadership styles are modifying to include more collaborative milieus. Technology has definitely impacted all brick and mortar operations and the need to consider an online presence as part of the 21st century business model has become essential to survival. Also, tele-medicine and remote triage is become the norm rather than the exception." Not to mention that thousands of new applications are introduced daily into the marketplace.

In order to get in the game, it takes courage (action despite fear), compassion, creativity, collaboration & commitment, as well as learning which automated or high-tech business model best serves your needs; and those that you will be serving through your product, goods, or service.

CHAPTER 2: I Don't Know How She Does It: Can Women Really Have It All?

Let's explore this question further...

The stage of this movie provides additional schemata themes for our discussion. Carrie Bradshaw, oh no, Sarah Jessica Parker, is portrayed as an upwardly mobile executive in a company, whose husband is a freelance architect. They have two young children. Sarah's character, Kate Reddy, for those of you who didn't get to watch the movie, is offered a killer job, but she already works over 70 hours a week, juggles her mothering responsibilities, albeit it poorly (as portrayed), and her husband picks up the slack for a period of time.

In the midst of Kate's competition for the promotion, her husband gains an out-of-the blue amazing project opportunity. He makes the sacrifice of postponing acceptance of the project, at risk of losing it, so that Kate can continue the pursuit of her dream job.

In another facet of the plot, Sarah's working counterpart (played by Pierce Bronson) Jack Abelhammer takes a liking to Kate and insists that she travel with him for business. This further widens the intimacy gap between Kate and her husband, which leads to jealousy and themes of impropriety.

At the end of the movie, Kate makes the choice to place her value for her family over her value of her dream job. Despite their marital struggles the couple romantically reconnects and realign their priorities regaining balance in their chosen dream life.

The themes that are represented in this movie are the choices made by women and men, who seek marriage and family, as well as, the challenges that arise from these choices, while attempting to grow professionally.

The myth of women seeking only providers in spouses is also dispelled.

A commonly held myth that household responsibilities cannot be shared through division of labor is addressed in a very exaggerated and humorous way. But the truth is the depiction of Sarah's character running out of the house with baby food on her business suit, and her daughter's barrette in her hair is pretty accurate of what can happen when you juggle the responsibilities of raising young children, maintaining a home, and one's profession.

Emerging themes that when disparity arises in marital relationships suspicions of infidelity, resentment, anger, and jealousy are unfortunately well portrayed in the movie.

Prince Charming or Charming Prince?

What comes to mind are little girls dreaming of their knight in shining armor, on their white horse, arriving right at the predestined moment, to sweep them off their feet and then they live happily ever after.

But no one ever shares what can happen in between.

Cue reality – You meet an attractive guy, who charms his way into your heart. You move in together, either physically or in your mind, and start playing house. You already have it all planned.

If you met in high school, you start off growing up together. If you met in college, you plan how to build your life together. And if you haven't met prince charming by graduation and you're headed into the workforce, get ready to play the field perhaps for a while.

In the first and second situations, you start the journey of finding yourself amidst beliefs of a need for a spouse, who will provide security. In the latter, you begin to worry that you must create your own security.

Single or married, who knows who is better off?

Cold facts of the status of marriage in the U.S. -- National Marriage and Divorce Rate Trends for 2010, indicate that there were 2,140,272 marriages as reported by 49 states, 6.9 per 1,000 population. The medium age of women getting married was 25.8. In 2014, the total USA population was roughly 3.9 million people.

The divorce rate as reported by 45 states was 3.2 per 1,000 population. Indicating a divorce rate of approximately 50%.

Trends in the current marital statuses of women using the 1982, 1995, 2002, and 2006–2010 NSFG indicated that the percentage of women who were in a first marriage at the time decreased over the past several decades, from 44% in 1982 to 36% in 2006–2010.

At the same time, the percentage of women who were cohabiting, increased steadily from 3.0% in 1982 to 11% in 2006– 2010. In addition, the proportion of women aged 15–44 who were never married at the time of interview increased from 34% in 1982 to 38% in 2006–2010.

These trends indicate that women were progressively seeking more autonomy and/or nontraditional relationships that were not intent upon formal legal marriage.

When we examined the variable of education during the same time. The proportion of women who were married for the first time increased with greater educational attainment from 37% among those without a high school diploma or General Educational Development high school equivalency diploma (GED) to 58% among those with a bachelor's degree and 63% of those with a master's degree or higher.

Further, the proportion of women who were cohabiting decreased as educational attainment increased. One in five (20%) women without a high school diploma or GED were currently cohabiting, while roughly 1 in 14 women (6.8%) with a bachelor's degree were currently cohabiting.

These statistics indicate that more women progressively are choosing to pursue higher learning in favor of getting married in early adult life, and if they do decide to get involved in a relationship, the more educated they are, the more likely they are to seek marriage. The average age of women getting married however increased, likely due to the increase incidence of cohabitation.

In conclusion, women are seeking higher education and less are getting married. And unfortunately, 50% of first time marriages are ending in divorce. Are these numbers in any way associated with more women seeking nontraditional roles and domains? Time will continue to tell the story.

Spouse versus Partner – Dispelling the myths associated with selection of life mates. Do we need both?

Young women spend a great majority of their time finding Mr. Right or Mr. Right Now. Once found, typically value is given to a man, who has all the prerequisites of our ingrained ideals. These are learned either from our mother's messages throughout childhood or from experience.

For example, he must have a particular physique (be active take care of himself), personality (expressive, great listener), treat us like queens and oh yes, we're going to say it, pay for dinner and open doors.

However, once the courtship has ended the very attributes that once made him so appealing, now are the most annoying. He gains weight, stops taking care of himself and you, he snores and it's no longer cute; and he assumes his role as financial provider and in some cases, not much else.

Or, as is a growing trend among our highly mobile girlfriends, he does not have a profession or steady income generating job that is commensurate to what you earn, but he does love you. Therefore, you convince yourself that his other attributes compensate for not making money towards the expenses of the household.

We must do a better job as mothers, to prepare the next generation of young women, to seek and to build relationships with their heart, yes, but also utilizing their minds. All too often, we can be led by only our hearts and pheromones.

In contrast seeking one's partner in life, requires self-compassion and a whole other set of skills. Yes, there must be physical attraction, but greater value has to be equally placed on a meeting of the mind and soul. There is a need for understanding each other's values, beliefs, skills set, hang-ups and backstories, in addition to matters of the heart and body.

Also, the secret ingredient to every lasting partnership is that there must be the belief of something greater than the two individuals in the relationship. The third that binds your marital relationship and makes it stronger than the individual two parts. We refer to it as, the threesome of all lasting marital relationships, you, your partner, and God.

Only then, can a partnership be entered into with fully open eyes. Not like some of our sisters, who do so with tightly closed eyes hoping for ecstasy and waking up to the realization that we attract exactly what we put out into the world and it was not what we thought or wanted.

Marriage is not a fantasy to be entered lightly, it is a lifelong commitment between two souls. It took us a long time to learn this life lesson, and several failed relationships, before we got it right.

The ingredients to a successful partnership are mutual respect, love and compassion, as well as maturity and a keen ability to actively listen to your partner and to complement each other, as needed. Because one thing is a certainty in marriage, challenges will come-up and when they do the romance between you may not be enough to weather the storm.

For example, as we are taking time on our islands (private offices) to write these words to share with you, our partners are picking up the slack in our households. Of course, we had the family meetings prior to taking on this adventure, in which we asked for their help in creating the time and space to permit us to create the content for this book.

It was only after gaining their respective buy-ins that we committed to one another that we would get this project done, because we all share the passion to uplift, teach and to mentor others to experience the fullness of life and vocation desired.

Children, family does it impact employability?

You and your partner are in marital bliss. You wake up one morning and decide the internal clock is ticking and it is time now to have a baby. You tell your husband, "Honey its time." Or you husband comes to you one afternoon, and says, "Honey don't you want a baby?"

Or your in-laws, best friends, or perfect strangers all start inquiring how long have you been married, when are you going to have kids?

Decision made, the blessing of conception happens. Now what? Waiting, waiting, and more waiting for the blessed event to occur, when you and your husband will add to your family.

No one really says it aloud, but during that waiting period, anxiety about, "Will we be able to afford childcare? Will that child take after my annoying sibling, or inherit my mother-in-law's nose? And please God let him or her be healthy" are the types of thoughts that consume the mind.

These thoughts dissipate the minute you see that little face, and then...the screeching wonderful sound of their cry.

Fast forward, now you have two children. Your nuclear family is complete. Your husband is working, but your job is tenuous, as you are plagued with fear of not wanting to leave your child, but also not wanting to lose your job. What do you do? Childcare in some cities is costlier than what the average women earns monthly.

Therefore, a choice must be made. You are not in the financial position to only have one income coming into the household, but does it make sense to pay out more than you earn. You discuss it with your husband and the decision is made. You will go out and seek better employment.

After distributing your resume with head hunters and placement consultants, you start to receive surmounting calls for interviews. This was Jessica's life 20 years ago, when she first relocated to South Florida. She had taken the time to prepare herself for her chosen profession, therefore she was confident that there was a better career and remuneration opportunity out there for her.

But she was in internal turmoil, "Do you do what is best financially for the family, or for your newborn?" The resonating voice of her mother in your head did not turn off. She was constantly being told, "Don't make the same mistake I made leaving you and your siblings alone, while I worked endless hours to provide for the five of you by myself. You are not in the same situation. Live with less and be home with your children."

But another voice that sounds very much like her own voice told her, "You devoted years to studies to be able to be a viable contributor to society. You have knowledge to share and for others to benefit from. How selfish is it that you not return to the labor force to share and help others?"

In an impulsive moment, she decided, "Okay I'll try staying home with my baby, after all she is very little and needs me." Jessica lasted exactly four months, breastfeeding, and attending mommy-and-me playdates with other new mothers, before she started calling her girlfriend to tell her that she thought she was losing her mind. Soon she shared that she could no longer hold an intelligent conversation, all she did was talk baby-talk. Now no offense meant, for those women, who were called to be stay-at-home mothers. We believe it is one of the hardest and least valued jobs in the world.

However, for Jessica, staying home resulted in falling into post-partum depression, gaining a lot of weight, and losing her identity.

After four months, her husband noticed the change in her, and he stated, "I can work part-time from home, or leave this job, and stay home with our baby." The words that came out of her husband's mouth were incredible.

Initially she thought that it was a dream. Then came the thought, "What kind of mother am I? That I would even consider leaving my baby girl to my husband, while I work?" But with minimal encouragement from him, she re-entered the labor force and her husband remained home with their child for the first year of her life. On lookers, thought and expressed, "What kind of relationship do you guys have?"

Her response, "A partnership." Over the last 20 years, Jessica and her husband have been supportive of each other's dreams and desires. It has been this give-and-take in their relationship that has allowed each of them to grow and to pursue their entrepreneurial ventures. They are now collaboratively raising two young ladies, who have been exposed, to what some might characterize as a nontraditional division of parental roles in the household.

As we explored the social context of marriage in the 21st century we found that the definition of marriage has evolved, due to the influence of politics. The definition of the word marriage—or, more accurately, the understanding of what the institution of marriage properly consists of—continues to be highly controversial. This is not an issue to be resolved by dictionaries.

Ultimately, the controversy involves cultural traditions, religious beliefs, legal rulings, and ideas about fairness and basic human rights. The principal point of dispute has to do with marriage between two people of the same sex, often referred to as same-sex marriage or gay marriage.

Same-sex marriages are now recognized by law in a growing number of countries and were legally validated throughout the U.S.

by the Supreme Court decision in Obergefell v. Hodges in 2015. In many other parts of the world, marriage continues to be allowed only between men and women. The definition of marriage shown here is intentionally broad enough to encompass the different types of marriage that are currently recognized in varying cultures, places, religions, and systems of law.

In the movie "I don't know how she does it," they tackle emerging themes when disparity arises in the couples' intimacy due to time constraints or work requirements that take Kate away from her family and gives rise to suspicions of infidelity, resentment, anger, and jealousy, which are some of the secondary challenges of women, who are increasingly participating in the workforce.

Wendy's experience was quite a bit different than the one Jessica mentioned earlier about her family life. Since she was never blessed with children, her career was always front and center. She has taken on many successful endeavors and had risen in leadership positions even when she didn't try. When she chose her significant others, (yes there were a few) there was never a doubt that she was to be the primary bread winner in the relationship. Her significant others acknowledged the fact that they would be taking the back seat to her career and for the most part knew what that might entail. Or so Wendy thought. Although the relationship roles appeared to be understood up front, consequences occurred during the span of the marriage(s) often resulting in not so good of results.

The pattern of choosing those that didn't quite understand Wendy's drive to achieve and lead was prevalent early on in her relationship history. Her very first boyfriend turned fiancé, turned out to be very jealous of her being around anyone but especially any other males. He never understood her want and need to lead and be out front and center of activities and events even though she was always loyal to him. He became very jealous and controlling of her every move. Throughout high school and then into her first year of college, any observation or report of her looking at or spending time with another man was considered an emotionally laden event with her being scolded and reprimanded for many days.

This co-dependent and emotionally abusive relationship created an impassable imprint on her ongoing relationships as she continued to pick partners that were not quite ready to accept the notion of her being focused on her career not being with them at all times and being at work all of the time or traveling away from home for work.

There were often disputes as to how often Wendy was working, what the expectations were around the house and how the traveling impacted the relationship. Themes of trust issues and jealousy were prevalent.

Unfortunately, the relationships often failed, leaving Wendy again with her career and trying to find someone that understood the passion for her work and her career without being threatened by her success. No one understood her need to be successful and prove her worth. She didn't realize that proving her worth in relationships was to be so difficult.

No matter what she attempted, it never appeared to be enough, and gave suspicion to the men who then would guiltily indicate that they would have to go elsewhere for love and compassion. Then at least one of them knowingly did. Manipulation was often the behavior used to explain why he was unfaithful. It really wasn't his fault, it was either Wendy's because she did not provide the appropriate level of attention, or when that didn't work anymore it was his mother's fault for rejecting him many times throughout his life.

Finally, when Wendy had enough and realized through a lot of counselling and help of her dear friend Jessica, that it wasn't her, she removed herself from the toxic relationship with great pain.

Wendy has now found that if you wait long enough you will find someone that truly understand your purpose and passion and is not threatened by your success. Wendy has found the person that not only encourages her in her ventures but also joins her in her vision to enhance the lives of others. They both value and share the household domain and their puppies, because they support each other's' work endeavors.

Marital partnerships require work, as well as tending and mending, at all times, if they are to last a lifetime. When imbalance in the relationship is encountered, communication is paramount. Underlying optimal communication is the evidence of maturity that must exist within the relationship. Learning how to communicate with your partner in a way that they can hear you is so vital. Also, recognizing that men and women communicate differently and being empathetic towards the differences is essential.

There are times when women speak of having outgrown their husband or vice versa, these are the seasons in life, when both partners have to lean in, and give of themselves unselfishly, to promote the other. Infidelity and jealousy are more symptoms of the condition of the individual than solely the condition of the marital relationship. The root of jealousy is insecurity.

Also, if infidelity occurs then the person, who falls short, is lacking something that is not being gained in the relationship or a result of self-harm. In most cases, it is a cry for attention among women. And for those of us that enter into relationships with traumatic pasts, it can be a byproduct of unconscious trauma memories that have not yet be healed.

We are complex emotional beings, women.

Over the years, the stories of marital difficulties that Jessica has heard in clinical practice have customarily been shared by individuals, who had not done their own self-work. Therefore, they were seeking to find themselves in their partner. This is never a good practice. Rather, partners need to complement one another.

In the movie, the supposition is that Sarah Jessica's character (Kate) was doing it all, albeit poorly, and something had to give. The truth of the matter is that to some extent, women, who chose to have a marital relationship, family, and career must master the art of task switching. It can be done, but not well all at the same time. That is why when a woman is in childbearing years, her body's hormonal make-up may signal the desire to have children, it is in this season that a choice has to be made.

In some cases, the conception of a child is not planned. In these circumstances, it is a difficult choice faced by a woman, who had not factored a child into her life plan.

In the movie, Kate choses to bow-out of the running for her dream job, in favor of her dream life with her husband and two children.

She is able to return to her career, although with imposed limits and boundaries to maintain her sanity.

The essential elements to sustaining this balancing act, is to have a partner, who is not leery of getting his hands dirty in household or childcare, and who respects your choice to pursue a career, as much as you respect his. Under these conditions, both spouses and the child(ren) can face life's challenges and opportunities as a team versus alone.

CHAPTER 3: The Proposal: The Millionaire-Made Entrepreneur™

Job description of self-description.
– Tim Ferriss (Thought Leader of the New Rich)

What if we told you, millions aren't what you really want?

What you want is the millionaire lifestyle. Or do you?

In the movie The Proposal, Sandra Bullock's classic Hollywood movie, plays an Editor of a large publishing house. She has a male assistant, who is from a very affluent family. The assistant has aspirations to make his mark in the publishing world on his own terms.

The protagonist played by Ryan Reynolds ridicules his boss for being such a 'ball buster', but he simultaneously admires her for standing her ground. Over the course of their working relationship, we are introduced to reverse gender bias in the work place.

As the audience, we observe as the protagonist's father, who wanted his son to pursue working the family business, does not believe that his son is simply the Editor's assistant, but that he must have another motive for their relationship, such as a romantic one.

The plot then thickens, where Sandra's character runs into a snag, when immigration services advised her that because she did not renew her visa, she must leave the country voluntarily, or be deported.

In order to remain in the country, she negotiates with her assistant, and coerces him to marry her for immigration status, in exchange, she agrees to his desired promotion.

However, the two fall in love in the process of the charade, even though their personalities were very different. Hers, the cold hard witch, who everyone is afraid of because she rules her department with a whip; and his, being one of the boys, a team player, who just plays the part of submissive in order to get access to what he wants from his boss. All the while, harboring his own secrets of a life of privilege.

Another layer of Sandra's character, as portrayed in the movie is that she has been so committed to her career that she sacrificed romance and relationships. All we know about the boss is that she is Canadian. We are not given any indication that she has family ties etc. The boss admits to her subordinate that she has even forgotten how to be intimate with a man. In fact, she discloses that it had been almost two years since she last had sex.

After some comic scenes of release in the movie, where Sandra's character learns, presumably, to bring down her guard and to integrate within her new family system has accidental physical interludes with Ryan's character, while attempting to maintain the charade, the movie draws to the end with the couple remaining together.

Although not specifically seen in the movie, Sandra's character presumably promotes her subordinate (as promised), before she leaves her post in the company. The sequel scene we profess is that Sandra's character, being proficient and skilled in her profession, seeks to establish her own publishing house, as she has a passion for the proliferation of literature/the written word.

This movie portrays several interesting themes pertaining to gender bias reversal, the perceived power of women in leadership, and what happens, when choice is not a factor in the equation.

There are also other themes in the movie that are supported by findings in the literature. The perception that women in power have to take on masculine characteristics (including making quick calls, taking action etc.) in order to be respected by subordinates and superiors in an organization is just one of them. Another theme is that there is a growing percentage of women, who are opting into the entrepreneur arena.

Enter the Rising Age of Women Entrepreneurs

In this book, we are using the definition of entrepreneur in the purer sense of the word, first coined by French economist J.B. Say, in the 1800's, "One who shifts economic resources out of an area of lower and into an area of higher yield."

Translation, is taking one's assets and converting them to the most optimal return on investment possible. Resources do not pertain only to money. They include who you know, what you know, and the know-how to use these skills, in addition to money, to accomplish your desired goals.

In her 20's, Jessica fell into (there is a reason for the use of these words, keep reading, you'll see why) creating a traditional brick and mortar company through entrepreneurship, due to the untimely disability of her mother. The only financial earner in her household, Jessica struck by an unwavering fear, immediately set her mind, to finding the gap in services within an arena she had been exploring for a year.

The way she and others, who worked for her at that time, describe this experience was that, "she was an unstoppable force, like a steaming train." She was unrelenting, worked creating for hours on end, she was obsessed in her focus to build a viable asset that would serve others and herself.

Within a few months, her start-up went from an owner/operator basement operation (where she and her mother were living), to three corporations employing over 100 people across three offices in a Metropolitan region.

Prior to this experience, Jessica knew nothing about business finance, operations or capitalization of ventures. But her Dr. J. Millionaire-Made Entrepreneur™ experience educated her quickly. She personally found passion to auto-educate herself in business finance, research, product/service development; but delegated operational management, accounting and IT within her organizations. Although her employees will attest, Jessica never took her eyes off the mark, she was a 'Tiger,' who defended her creations, and mentored us in the process (Viviana Malamud, former employee of Rehab Alert Enterprises, Inc.).

Over the following years, Jessica found herself in a position she never dreamed, she owned and operated three multimillion dollar revenue producing corporations, was paid to talk on prestigious stages, was a guest on televised programs; and was named Latin Female Entrepreneur at the ripe age of 25.

She got to live the millionaire lifestyle and learned many life lessons in the process at a young impressionable age. The ones that stood out the most at the time were how money can influence, what it means to be a woman in a leadership position, and how unfortunate it can be when our inner mindset is set on self-sabotage.

Jessica describes her personal experience during this time in her life as, "It was as though a dormant gene was ignited in me, and that from that date on fuels my passions for self-compassion, empowering of others, and business creation." But, and yes there is a but in her story, or rather her backstory, that her co-workers and employees never knew of at the time. Her inner thoughts were riddled with pain, insecurities, and FEAR.

Over the next three decades, Jessica would devote her life to working through her inner mind field blocks, clearing and purging trauma memories, through self-work and learning. The result a Ph.D. in psychological, human applied sciences, and in the process, she helped hundreds of thousands of people in pain (of all sorts) find peace with their past. And for those with an interest, she mentored them to use what they learned from their past, to position them to flourish, in their present through entrepreneurship. It is her life work.

However, just like in the various movies reviewed in this book, there were sacrifices that she made. For many years, she put off personal relationships and family in favor of her career. When she did meet, her partner in life, and they decided to have a family, she made the decision to step-out of her role of entrepreneur (for a season) and to step into motherhood and traditional employment.

It was during this season in life that Jessica and Wendy met.

Wendy was, at the time, an upwardly striving rehabilitation specialist, who had been formally trained in Speech Language Pathology and Audiology. However, she did not remain in the therapist role very long into her career. Wendy had a keen eye for opportunity for advancement within the corporate arena.

Wendy made her way through the ranks quickly, while initially as a lead therapist, within a short span of time, she ascended into the c-suite. One former coworker, Marla, recalls, "Working with Wendy was always a positive experience. She never micromanaged and valued me and my skills. She was always thankful for my timely work and inspired me to work harder. Most importantly she made me feel that she cared about me and supported my ideas and my professional goals. She is at the top of the list of the best managers I ever worked for."

Marla also shared that that one of her fondest memories with Wendy, was when she stayed with her at the hospital, after Marla was badly injured in a car accident and helped Marla to get FMLA so she could keep her job. Marla stated, "I will never forget your kindness."

It appeared, that no ceiling existed for Wendy. It was not until she reached her pinnacle position within HealthSouth, as one of the highest paid Directors of Clinical Services and Operations (excluding finance and nursing components) in Rehabilitation, that she experienced her first blow that is commonly shared by most female leaders in organizations.

The ceiling in the organization's structure shifted and her position was eliminated. A secondary cultural factor, she recalls was that her position was amidst a predominantly Hispanic male-run division. She was given an "out", a new opportunity in Arkansas. This position however required relocation to an unfamiliar area, and a minimum 3 year commitment... for the same, and possibly less pay.

This setback in Wendy's career plan did not stop her from pursuing her career goals. She quickly gathered her assets, and began the hunt for a new corporate opportunity. Wendy had always been an overachiever, and soon found herself in the leadership position she had originally sought. She was hired as a Division Vice President of Clinical Services, for a principle player in the rehabilitation medical field... remaining in the city she had come to call home.

It was within this organization that Wendy and Jessica met and got their first taste of what it means to work collaboratively with another entrepreneurial woman. It was a fascinating time. Both women were learning their way through the organizational culture, building strategic relationships and accumulating resources. They recognized that each brought unique skills sets and strengths to the table, but also that their differences could be leveraged to propel them both out of Corporate America.

In the span of just two years, the corporation they were working for was acquired and merged with other entities several times. It was characteristic of economic trends of the time. Wendy experienced her second divorce, finding Mr. Right Now in the process, and Jessica grappled with the challenges of juggling her role as wife, mother, and corporate employee.

Eventually, Wendy's division was dissolved and then Jessica got the "itch". That innate prompting that it was time to get back into the entrepreneurial arena. Timing was favorable for both ladies. The result, a partnership was co-founded, as well as a consulting agency, Care Access Enterprises, Inc.

CAE immediately landed several significant contracts, initially within the healthcare arena (Bally's, CyberCare, CORF America etc...) and then abroad with McLarens Adjusters Canada etc. in disability claims management/rehabilitation. The ladies were traveling a great deal, which took them away from their families. They made the conscious decision to not become top-heavy as an organization therefore their resource structure remained owner-operator.

Although things were going well, travel had become a huge burden on the two of them. Wendy was traveling from Arizona, Jessica from Florida to fulfill all of the contracts they had. Knowing that they each needed to slow down and enjoy things, they decided to dissolve CAE (for the moment). Wendy decided to remarry and rejoin corporate America by converting one of her contracts to employment, Jessica pregnant with her second child, was defending her dissertation and preparing for her family.

Logistically, the above factors lent themselves to the ladies' pursuit of different life paths for a time. However, their lifelong friendship and partnership continues, as they are the co-founders of the 'YaYa' sisterhood. A community of women leaders, who are spirited entrepreneurs from all walks of life that recognize that we are stronger working together, than against each other.

The Economic Tide Changer

Most corporate ladder climbers, brick and mortar operators, homemakers and self-employed women share one misnomer. They, and the population at large continue to focus on the old ways to achieve wealth, prestige, power, title and maintain the belief that if you work hard it will pay off.

According to author and high-tech entrepreneur, Tim Firress, (author of the 4-Hour Work Week, who has coined the terminology 'New Rich) being rich has nothing to do with money. And, traditionalist, who have chosen the 9-5 or beyond jobs need to pause and reflect, because finding oneself in the majority, may in fact mean lacking imagination and the ability to take advantage of new opportunities (Mark Twain and Oscar Wilde).

In Firress' New Rich economy, the desired commodities are; time, mobility, flexibility, and choices. Needed resources are only as valuable as one's lifestyle choices.

Let's face it, as women with multidimensional desires that span across self, family, marital relationships, friendships, career, community and causes that stir our hearts, sometimes simultaneously; the perfect job we need to have is the one that takes the least time.

Because the truth is that there is no job that provides unending fulfillment, so we have to shift our mindset to one that serves to free time and automates income, as much as possible. That is the ultimate truest outcome of entrepreneurship.

The New Rich generation seemingly is comprised of millennial tech and innovative entrepreneurs, who have learned or are learning to leverage the power of a Wi-Fi connection and the internet (high-tech entrepreneurship). However, observation of the landscape reveals that evolving Gen X and Baby Boomers, who have hacked the code to live the millionaire's lifestyle, have reengineered previously universal beliefs about work and money, in order to prosper in this new age of technology.

According to Firress, if we really reflect, we are not too interested in earning six, seven, or eight figures annually, but rather living the lifestyles of those who have that type of fluidity of resources. Let's take a peek at a few examples:

A young man in his mid to late twenties, whom we recently met during travels abroad, told of his story of selling all of his worldly possession to fund his dream to travel to an exotic location in Asia. He wanted to experience self-exploration, and to ultimately train and compete in a unique form of martial arts... not really knowing what he might be doing for shelter and food.

Unfortunately, in this example, the young man, from our vantage point, was jumping off the cliff, without a parachute. His plan involved physical and mental training, to then potentially engaging in fights to earn sufficient money in hopes of making his way back to civilization one day. Is this what is meant to be in the New Rich? We would consider this an example of a nomad and rebel, who is broke.

Utilizing the paradigm shift in business, suggested by the New Rich culture, if this young man, were to have established an online presence with a product or service that is scalable, with minimal personal touch points, and produced automated residual income before he took his leap of faith into marital arts, then yes, he is in the "in."

Here is another example. We recently learned of a stay-at-home mother, who made top billing in the media briefly for her great entrepreneurial idea. Her husband lost his job, fell into depression, and she was left to raise and provide for the family, with limited presumed resources. While watching the coverage of the presidential election, this mom overheard a candidate's campaign slogan, became passionate about taking it and creating something to promote empowerment of the people, because she was tired of all the media negativity. She took the family's last financial resources, created her own website, produced t-shirts with her play of the words from the candidate's slogan and launched her goods on the internet. Within 24-hours this woman created a media frenzy, sold all her t-shirts, and gained several thousand orders for more. This venture produced a sell-out launch and an undisclosed exorbitant amount of money for her family within weeks.

What do you think she felt like in that moment? Is she a Dr. J. Millionaire-Made Entrepreneur™ and/or in the New Rich culture?

Stories like both of these are constantly in the media today. You just have to open up your browser or mailbox and you'll find that whatever you were perusing the day before, now mysteriously sits in the margin of your screen. Images of those exact shoes or clothing item you wanted, or the vacation destination, or anything else searched for on the web.

Technology has gotten so sophisticated that one does not even have to be a programmer/coder anymore. Rather there is software for everything and, if you cannot find it, then you can create it. Tech based millionaires are the boy or girl next door, who got an idea, established a web presence and started marketing it. Presto product launches generating hundreds of thousands, if not millions of dollars on the web. Just open your email and among the many spam emails there you will find one or more emails from individuals, who are selling something, after making millions in just six months.

After the movie, Social Media was released, 100's of thoughts of New Rich were created. Although this is true, we believe that the special sauce to entrepreneurship on or offline has a 97% rate of failure in the first two years (for small businesses). Primarily due to a lack of scalability and a lust for solely money.

In contrast if you set out with a higher purpose, calling or mission, like eradicating human exploitation, then your business model grows itself as momentum is gained for the greater good of others. There is something very motivating about knowing that every day that you delay in pushing out your new business product or service, is another day that a child is in the hands of a monster.

Also, too many people accept failure, and shut down their business, instead of leaning in and using the failure to find the next solution. Fear and Faith do not make good bedfellows.

The Age of Tech, The New Rich, & Women Entrepreneurial Pain Points Revealed

In an online article in the Business Insider, 2010 the title read, "Let's be Real about the Lack of Women in Tech." That title caught our eye, then when we learned that the commentary was provided by **Fred Wilson (male perspective)** of Union Square Venture on Change the Ratio, being interviewed by Rachel Skylar we knew it had to be included here.

The findings in the article resonated with the top pain points identified by a whopping 90% of random women anecdotally surveyed in 2016; fear of use of technology as an obstacle to pursuit of entrepreneurship online. The article actually offers seven (7) reasons for the lack of women in tech:

1. Lack of Role Models - Joanna Krotz writes in Microsoft Business, "We're now experiencing the first generation or so of widespread success for women-owned businesses. That means the been-there/done-that part of the mentor equation isn't as deep or wide for women as it is for men. That holds true for mentors and entrepreneurs alike."

2. Women Need Mentors, but Women Don't Always Mentor Other Women - By nature, women are stand-offish towards their sex. Catherine Kaputa, author of The *Female Brand: Using the Female Mindset to Succeed in Business,* writes, "Men are much more likely to help anyone, even someone they barely know. Women think they need to know someone fairly well in order to help them, so women don't have as many contacts as men."

Phillis Chesler, author of, *Women Inhumanity to Women agrees:* "Women rarely admitted that they themselves are harder on women than on men, that they hold higher and different standards for women than they do for men, and that they often never forgive each other [for things they] routinely forgive men [for]."

3. Women Like to Talk - We're stereotyped as complainers. What separates entrepreneurs from everyone else, not just from women, is that they **execute** their ideas; they don't just talk about them.

4. Women have Timers - Medicine has made it possible for women to start families at later ages. But biologically, women have only a few prime years.

Wilson has seen this happen to female entrepreneurs' first-hand. "My wife, The Gotham Gal -- she was a great entrepreneur, but she wanted to have a family, and then she had to stay at home. That was a big gulf in her career."

So, what's the solution? Wilson says, "A lot of it is about getting the word out that women can [start companies right away]. The times to do it are right out of college, when they have low burn rate, or later when their family can afford to take a financial risk."

5. Women are Averse to Risk - Women, by nature, are more calculated than men, which can inhibit them from taking the entrepreneurial plunge.

TechCrunch's Michael Arrington referenced a conversation with Cyan Banister, co-founder of Zivity: "Women are nurturing and not risk-taking enough by nature...When men roll the dice and take risks, society doesn't punish them at all, and it's in their nature to take stupid risks." While this quality benefits women in many ways, it can keep them from becoming entrepreneurs.

6. Venture Capitalists (VC) are White Arrogant Males - VCs invest in what they know-- and what they don't know is women. Founders tend to start companies based on topics that interest them. The problem is, a lot of what interests' women doesn't interest male investors. "If the tech industry is going to be dominated by men, then we're going to get services that target that crowd," says Wilson. "Let's take the fashion sector for example. It's a hard sector for me to evaluate." Wilson says he wears the same outfit every day. He elaborates, saying he doesn't know where the value in the fashion industry lies - is it in manufacturing, distribution or retail? And if you don't know where the value in an industry is, then how can you make an investment? "It's a challenge for us as investors. I definitely think that makes it hard for women entrepreneurs who are passionate about sectors that are difficult for men like me to evaluate."

7. Entrepreneurship Was Never Cool Until Now - Until Sergey Brin, Larry Page and Mark Zuckerberg, the only people creating companies were small mom and pop shops, and uber computer nerds. Now, that's all changing.

People see entrepreneurship as the modern-day lottery. Wilson references The Social Network saying, "Thousands of people will go out and start companies because of that movie." He claims his kids were immediately more interested in his job after they saw the flick. It's safe to assume there's never been more interest in entrepreneurship, among men and women alike.

Like the **Editor** in the **Proposal**, let's be **Real** about the **Unchanged Perception** of **Women** and **Leadership**

The literature is vast, so for our purposes we are going to limit the findings to the following assumptions, as found in literature (see reference addendum) that relates to our discussion of why the portrayal in media and the perpetuated perception of women in leadership **has not** changed much in the last several decades:

The Biological Assumption – This assumption rests on the notion that men and women are different. They are built differently, they think differently, they behave differently. The basic premise under this assumption is that "leadership is biologically determined." These references note that women's linguistic styles constitute another language for many men and that these styles are often "devalued by men". However, the premise of biologically determined leadership cannot be deduced from the existence of markedly different linguistic styles. Studies that were reviewed that operate from this theoretical framework investigate the deficiencies of female leadership. **An implication is made that acquiring male leadership values, qualities, and skills are necessary to succeed in leadership.**

The Sociological Assumption - Despite sweeping socio-political changes in the last forty years, significant sociological assumptions continue to deter, if not prevent, success for females in the executive echelons of business. It appears that the last half decade of reforms has not been accompanied by marked changes in gender stereotyping. Social role and expectation theory are rooted in sociological assumptions: "individuals react to leaders with gendered expectancies...in return, leaders respond because of their internalized gender role." Studies that operate from the sociological theoretical framework investigate the sociological drivers for leadership and provide evidence that significant social change is necessary to facilitate female leadership success. Aspiring female leaders may be forgiven, however, for asking the question, "Now what?"—the sociological framework leaves little hope, much less direction, for women aspiring to leadership positions today or in the near future.

Structural/Cultural Assumption - Researchers have argued that masculinity and femininity are defined culturally rather than sociologically or biologically. Arguing from a feminist mode of inquiry, it is proposed that structural and cultural assumptions "reproduce global inequalities." Studies that operate from this theoretical framework investigate the organizational and cultural drivers of leadership. Within this framework, women are typically expected to "cultivate more masculine methods" to fit in an organizationally or culturally predefined male leadership model.

Line Experience Assumption – Purports that it appears that many would-be female executives are caught in the "experience wanted" trap: line experience is valued but all too often not made available to female managers aspiring to executive status. Other research, indicates that the "scarcity of female corporate officers is the sum of discrimination that has operated at all ranks."

From these assumptive positions, it appears that the emergence of a feminine leadership style is bleak. Particularly since well into the 20th century gender perceptions about leadership style persisted; albeit, some distinction started to be recognized and valued, such as female leadership style tends to be transformational while male leadership style tends to be transactional. Women are communal, with associated nurturing and facilitative behaviors while male leadership styles are typically described as agentic with behaviors associated with achievement behaviors.

Jacobs, describes gender leadership dynamic as "Men think 'can do, will do' while women think 'have done, will do'". These gender stereotypes contribute to considerable barriers to female leadership.

Exploring the Female Leadership Advantage Perspective

Some theorists suggest that the female advantage perspective is beginning to mitigate the barriers to female leadership by claiming that traditional masculine styles of leadership are being discarded and that new millennial models "synchronous with feminine ways are becoming desirable". However, some note that the "choice to move too far within or outside feminine social constructions can be detrimental to the perceived competence of the woman's leadership."

The key, which is gaining momentum in the 21st century, is that there is no right way to lead, whether masculine or feminine, just the right way for the culture being created. And the culture of entrepreneurial organizations today is more and more being created by women for women and by evolving men with women, who recognize the importance of not excluding or ostracizing 50% of the population, and more importantly, the largest segment of the consumer market.

The 'What' Women Can Bring to the Table

We are not trying to man-bash in any regard. If you haven't realized by now let us spell it out, we believe that both genders have that special something in them universally, that when we work collectively can create magic. But, all too often in our society, cultures, and in business one part of the equation is missing, undervalued or not heard, WOMEN. And we as women do not do a good job of promoting, equipping and collaborating with each other. One of our calls is to change that by reengineering the status quo.

4 Principle Assets Women Leaders Bring to the Table

1. **Pragmatic Intuitive Problem Solving**: We can integrate facts and the experience of human resources to propose alternate solutions, by identifying gaps, rather than solely based upon data.

2. **Promote Collaboration**: By recognizing the importance of valuing others and what they have to offer, actively listening, then strategic planning that is collective rather than solely directive, is achieved. Still with the end goal in mind. Our unique linguistic style lends itself to building trusting teams.

3. **Master Tasker**: Leveraging our biology in favor of working on multiple moving parts of a project, we have the unique ability of switching from task to task efficiently, giving concerted attention to each, and pushing out multifaceted creations.

4. **Consumer Pulse**: Unlike men, who are immediate action takers, as the clear majority consumer, we uniquely bring that consumer perspective to the table and consider it, when developing product/services, we have our finger on the pulse, and typically innovatively offer alternatives to gain desired outcomes. Failure being a stepping stone to the next solution.

Barriers Still Faced by Women Leaders

We have found that common stereotypic presumptions continue and unfortunately serve to perpetuate the status quo, but we know otherwise and promote others.

Just for informational purposes these are a few of them:
1. Women lack ambition
2. Women don't have the right work experience
3. Women don't have the leadership skills.

4. Women don't have the problem-solving skills

5. Women won't make the necessary sacrifices.

Other contributing factors

1. Lack of access to informal networks

2. Lack of mentors

3. Lack of access to influential colleagues

4. Lack of role models

5. Lack of stretch assignments

6. Limited flexible work arrangements

Solution, the writing of this book and more of them, to inform and enlighten our sisters, to make a change, band together, and to uplift each other.

Geri Stengel, contributing author, wrote in Forbes Magazine 2016 recently wrote, "There is an increasing percentage of women owned businesses 36% in 2012, a 30% increase over 2007." These numbers are a staggering 30 percent growth in the last decade more than in the last 100 years of women in history.

In Stengel's article, she also brings up a common pain point for women, FINANCE (as it pertains to entrepreneurial ventures).

Sharon Vosmek (an economist and CEO of Astia – a nonprofit organization that identifies and propels high-potential women-led companies with expertise and money) wrote that the biggest challenge women face when starting and growing their businesses is access to capital, especially equity financing.

Female entrepreneurs start companies with 50% less capital than male entrepreneurs, according to Access to Capital by High-Growth

Women-Owned Businesses research commissioned by the National Women's Business Council (NWBC).

Jessica, Wendy and many other women-led company owners they have met throughout the years attest to this experience. Jessica recalls that when she started her businesses and approached a traditional bank for a loan, she was flatly turned down. She was told, "You are too young, inexperienced, you must know that small business fail 90% of the time in the first year. You have no assets of value that we can lean against, if you default. Sorry, No!" She recalls that she heard 'No' so many times that she stopped seeking bank financial backing.

However, years into her businesses, after creating financial resource, she went to a bank and spoke to the manager, who happened to be a female. Jessica recalls, "It was such a different experience. This time, the bank manager, seeing all the fluidity in the accounts, immediately offered to bank roll a new venture spinoff from the principle company." This experience left Jessica with the sense that, once one provides 'proof of solvency' then there are banks that will work with you.

A Golden Age for women entrepreneurs is evolving in 2017

Carla Harris, NWBC's chair, a nonpartisan federal advisory council was quoted as stating, "We believe that today provides a perfect opportunity, a perfect storm if you will, for women entrepreneurs. Interest rates are at record lows, creating a robust environment for commercial borrowing. Record levels of cash are on the sidelines with both institutional and individual investors and on corporate balance sheets. And all of these entities are looking for good ideas, particularly as the appetite for risk continues to increase in the market."

Entrepreneurs start companies when they see a need in the marketplace that they can fill, whether it is creating a new product or service or targeting an underserved segment of the market.

According to the 2015 Kauffman Index; Startup Activity, "Women entrepreneurs are more adept than their male counterparts at seeing gaps in the market and seizing the opportunity."

Pamela Prince Eason, president and CEO of Women's Business Enterprise National Council (WBENC) was quoted as stating in a 2016 review, "WBEs [women business enterprises] are agile, innovative problem-solvers, meeting corporations' needs quickly, adapting to marketplace changes and providing deep value and cost-effectiveness."

Sallie Krawcheck, CEO of Ellevest and chairman of Ellevate wrote, "2016 will be the year in which the forces of entrepreneurialism and feminism converge. Together, they will drive a long-wave, golden age of female entrepreneurship, which will be a positive for all of us: positive and empowering for the women who make the leap, good for the economy, good for consumers, and good for society."

Women have to become better informed capitalist;
Snap shot of signs of change in the venture capital industry

The truth – women remain limited in their access to venture capital for the very reasons previously outlined in this and the former chapters - presumptive gender biases about women and their abilities in business.

However, we too cannot put all the blame on others, we have to recognize that as women we have customarily been the money managers in the households, responsible for budgeting and spending. Therefore, innately well-educated to further our knowledge when considering the leap into entrepreneurship. If you glaze over when reading the proceeding sections, our advice is get a few books on the topic, find a mentor or training program and learn all you can, because understanding finance, economic trends is not only relevant for business, it is relevant for your life and the future wellbeing of your children and their futures.

Let us provide the distinction between the types of investors. Angel Investors, or informal investors are, "Affluent individuals who inject capital for startups in exchange for ownership equity or convertible debt. Typically, they invest in small startups or entrepreneurs. Often, angel investors are among an entrepreneur's family and friends. The capital angel investors provide may be a one-time investment to help the business propel or an ongoing injection of money to support and carry the company through its difficult early stages. Angel investors must meet the Securities Exchange Commission's (SEC) standards for accredited investors. To become an angel investor, one must have a minimum net worth of $1 million and an annual income of $200,000. The internal rate of return for an Angel Investor is typical 20-30%."

In contrast Venture Capitalist are, "investors who either provide capital to startup ventures or support small companies that wish to expand but do not have access to equities markets. Well-known venture capitalists include Jim Breyer, an early Facebook investor, Peter Fenton, an investor in Twitter, Peter Theil, the co-founder of PayPal and Facebook's first investor, Jeremy Levine, the largest investor in Pinterest, and Chris Sacca, early investor in Twitter and ride-share company Uber. Venture capitalists look for a strong management team, a large potential market and a unique product or service with a strong competitive advantage. They also look for opportunities in industries that they are familiar with, and the chance to own a large percentage of the company so that they can influence its direction."

When you are looking for vehicles to capitalize your venture, do the research because most women seek to start-up companies based upon their passions and interests, they do not apparently relate well in terms of translation into financial prospects for VC, who are still primarily male.

Nisa Amoils, an active Angel Investor, reported her opinion that when VCs take an interest in your company, there is still the risks associated with "Money from venture capitalist's scales disrupting products and services." She goes on to reiterate that, "We cannot afford to leave out half the population developing future innovations (women). But you can't improve what you don't measure."

Kay Koplovitz, chairman and cofounder of Springboard Enterprises, an accelerator for women-led businesses in technology, media, and life sciences, provided promising stats of the growing presence of women in arena writing that, "According to CB Insight's 2014, 17% of the top 20 Corporate VC firms had women on the investment team versus 11% of Top 20 VC list. Since women VCs are more inclined to see the value in a women-led enterprise, this shift bodes well for women entrepreneurs. I am also encouraged that nine of Forbes' 30 Under 30 Top Young Investors of Venture Capital in 2016 are women."

By taking chances and gaining visibility, women in business are turning the tide, albeit slowly. The key is to become informed of the various vehicles, other than traditional start-up loans available to women-owned businesses. Some argue also that it would behoove us to encourage more women to seek careers in finance and for those who have resources to invest in their sisters.

Creating more Women Angel Investors and Ways to Connect Women to Investors

The changes in women getting funding from Angels is improving, but despite it, it is nowhere near commensurate with our male counterparts. While the number of female accredited investors (a.k.a wealthy people) becoming angels has increased dramatically

–one in four angels are now women -- more fuel is needed. And it's on its way. Organizations to help women become angel investors are springing up (See Resource List).

If you are not an upwardly mobile affluent person, or you don't have an appetite for the risk associated with equity investing then know that debt products are available under Title III of the JOBS Act (See Resource List).

Vosmek states, "Women alone can't solve the underfunding of women, men still control the vast majority of investments. Men need to ask themselves tough questions. Why do I have so few women-led companies in my portfolio? Is it how I source companies and network?" Then they can address their own hidden bias.

While angel and venture backed women-led companies get the headlines, America's future runs through Main Street, writes Maria Contreras-Sweet who heads the Small Business Administration. Small business activity for nearly all 50 states and the top 40 metropolitan areas is on the rise, according to Kauffman's Main Street Entrepreneurship Index. Women are one reason for the growth.

Creating even more and deeper pools of money

The stats in traditional vehicles for capitalization are also on the rise for women. Women-owned businesses are receiving more traditional loans, particularly from the SBA, according to 10 Million Strong: The Tipping Point for Women's Entrepreneurship NWBC's annual report. The SBA made $3.8 billion in capital available to women. Lending to women is up to 36%, increasing 19 percentage points, according to the SBA Office of Capital Access.

The tides in our economy have set the stage for further innovations in contraction in funding. These options fall into three categories:

online marketplace lenders, rewards-based crowdfunding, and equity-based crowdfunding.

Online Marketplace lenders provide simplicity and convenience in applying, a quick decision on loan approval, speedy delivery of capital and a greater focus on customer service. Applications can be completed in fewer than 30 minutes, compared to the 24 hours typical for the traditional bank application process, according to the Joint Small Business Credit Survey Report 2014.

Morgan Stanley estimates marketplace lenders will grow from 2% of loans to small businesses (approximately $5 billion) in 2014 to 16% in 2020. "[Women] are typically owner-operators, so they often don't have the time to fill out the lengthy and cumbersome application at the bank, or to wait the weeks it takes them to get approved, said Candace Klein, chief strategy officer of Deal stuck, "Because online marketplace lenders look at a number of online and offline factors to determine financing eligibility, accept creative forms of collateral, and move quickly in offering funds, even women with moderate to low credit scores may qualify for growth capital. They are filling a need for debt financing that banks aren't able to fill." For an analysis of some online marketplace lenders, go to NerdWallet.

Don't glaze over on us. The trick here is to get up walk about for a few minutes and then return and get back into the content. When we first had to learn this believe us, it was all Chinese, but if you have a passion, then you have a start-up idea and we want you to join the Dr. J. Millionaire-Made Entrepreneur™ Incubator Challenge. Make your dream a reality.

Rewards-based crowdfunding provides debt- and equity-free money.

You don't need to give up a piece of your company in exchange for the money or pay interest on a loan. However, you do need to give something tangible in exchange for someone's money. That could be pre-invoicing the product, selling it at a discount before it is manufactured, or offering a token gift, such as a t-shirt. Websites, such as Indiegogo, Kickstarter, and Plum Alley, coordinate the transactions.

To be successful, reward campaigns take a lot of hard work as well as marketing dollars. Women are proving that they have the right stuff to be successful at reward campaigns. Women had a 70% success rate in reaching their goals on Kickstarter vs. 61% for men, with further analysis showing that it was not women's more modest financial goals that accounted for their higher rate of success, according to research conducted by Hebrew University, the Kauffman Foundation, and UC Berkeley.

To learn more on equity-based crowdfunding includes three forms covered by the JOBS Act (Title II, Title III and Title IV) and intrastate crowdfunding please see Resource List.

The power of media. Stories in the media inspire and hold bad players accountable

Media play an important role in inspiring entrepreneurship and providing a road map. High-visibility stories about women who have succeeded big time or are on the rise is a testament to the public's appetite for this information.

Women entrepreneurs are not just making headlines they're making it on

The Forbes 2016 World's 100 Most Powerful Women List. These women became celebrities because they built empires.

Among these the top five were;

5th, Marry Barra, CEO, GM US,

4th Melinda Gates, Co-Chair, The Bill and Melinda Gates Foundation,

3rd Janet Yellen, Chair Federal Reserve US,

2nd Hillary Clinton, First, First Lady to as Presidential Candidate; and

1st Angela Merkel, Chancellor Germany.

These aren't the only women in the headlines. TechCrunch prepared a list of female founders who've made a major dent on tech. Check out their list of 18 Female Founders Who Killed it in 2015 (https://techcrunch.com/gallery/21-female-founders-who-killed-it-in-2015/slide/5/).

Hear women leaders of middle-market companies Roar

Women-owned/led business now account for 13% of middle-market firms (companies with revenues between $10 million and $1 billion). Companies run by women are entering the middle market at rates eight times of businesses in general. While the number of middle-market firms grew by 4% between 2008 and 2014, the number of women-owned/led firms increased by 32%.

Marsha Firestone, president and founder of the WPO recently stated, "Ten years ago, 7% of WPO member businesses had revenues of $10 million. Today, one quarter of our membership is at $10 million or more in revenue."

Closing the wealth gap

Not all metrics about women-owned businesses are positive. These firms generate only 11% of the combined revenues of businesses and women are less likely to have employees than in the past, according to NWBC's analysis of 2012 Census.

The percent of employer firms that are women-owned businesses decreased from 2007 to 2012 and the decline was steepest among African-American and Hispanic women-business owners. Employer firms represent 11% of all women-owned firms, 3% of African American women-owned firms and 5% of Hispanic women-owned firms.

Many women-owned businesses are struggling and this is cause for concern. Necessity entrepreneurs are far less likely to be successful than entrepreneurs who start businesses to pursue an opportunity, which tends to be the case when examining the stats on minority women owned businesses. However, this was not Jessica's experience or that of many aspiring entrepreneurs who have a passion, identified a gap-need, and are creative enough to fill it, in an equitable manner.

There are also city-based organizations who are seeing this gap in capitalization of minority-led entrepreneurship and are taking an invested interest to help. Women Entrepreneurs NYC (WE NYC) is a first-of-its kind model in a major American city for empowering women through entrepreneurship. They recognized that to achieve their potential, low-income, immigrant women needed support. Alicia Glen (Deputy Mayor for housing and economic development) stated, "The City wanted to make the most impact by addressing the biggest opportunities and biggest market failures.

These women face a society (and maybe even their own internal voices) that, by and large, say 'you can't do it'. WE NYC will address the confidence gap by demystifying business planning and financing through training, mentoring and networking events in neighborhoods across the five boroughs. In addition, the City is also evaluating creating a financing vehicle to address the needs of women raising between $25,000 and $250,000. The program has already inspired Boston to do something similar."

Corporations and government agencies can play an important role in growing women's businesses

"One of the biggest problems women have is getting access to new markets," said Firestone, who is also president of Women Presidents' Educational Organization, a regional certification provider for the WBENC. "Certification allows women [who own at least 51% of their business] to get markets they never dreamed of reaching before. If it wasn't for certification, they never could have grown their revenues to the degree that they now are."

"Corporate America has a very large role to play in entrepreneurship," said Nina Vaca, author of "Forget the Glass Ceiling: Build Your Business Without One". Vaca is founder and CEO of Pinnacle Technical Resources, an IT staffing and Technology Company. Her company was #1 on WPO's 50 Fastest-Growing Women-Owned/Led Companies on the list. Her company is approaching a billion in sales. Vaca was referring to the importance of certification in helping open doors to corporate and government contracts for women-owned companies.

Nina Vaca also commented that, "Corporations can provide money and expertise to grow women's businesses big. Corporate Venture and sponsorship of accelerators and incubators is on the rise, but there is plenty of room for growth and exciting ways this can be combined with crowdfunding".

Middle market companies have a role to play too. They can be a strategic investor. Jewel Burks, co-founder and CEO of Partpic, uses object recognition software to identify missing or damaged parts, such as screws, so the manufacturer can send a replacement. Robert Saunders, whose family owns Xander Fasteners, became a strategic investor and her first customer.

Another creative way to get involved according to Amois is, "Corporations looking to dip their toe into venture capital, can become a limited partner in a venture capital firm that invests in women-led companies,"

Moving beyond mentorship and support to investment

Mentorship and support is great, but money is way better. "This is THE missing piece for women," said Vosmek. Whether it is attracting or retaining talent or supporting women entrepreneurs, many corporations claim women are a top priority, but don't back up their words with money.

More corporations need to recognize the value of supporting women: It improves their own bottom lines. Investing in women entrepreneurs gives them access to products and services that better meet the needs of businesses and consumers. Women-friendly companies also benefit from increased brand loyalty from women, who make more than 80% of consumer purchase decisions in this country.

Money is out there. Corporations are sitting on cash. Family offices, foundations, endowment funds, retirement funds and even wealthy individuals could invest in VCs whose partners are diverse or funds that target investing in women-led companies. More male angel investors could invest in – and not just say they support – women-led companies. Not because it's the right thing to do, but because they'll make more money.

Women have more than proven their abilities. Research from Dow Jones, Kauffman and the SBA showing not just good performance but out performance of women-led companies compared to all-male teams. The latest is published by First Round, a venture capital firm, which found that female-founded companies they funded performed 63% better than all-male founding teams.

Even sharks recognize the outsized returns women deliver. "One hundred percent of my returns the last six years have come from companies run by women," said Kevin O'Leary, entrepreneur and Shark Tank investor, in Forbes "...So this year on Shark Tank, I'm investing in a lot of women."

In just two generations, women have gone from owning 5% of businesses in 1972 to 38% of businesses. In 2016, 11.3 million women-owned businesses generated $1.6 trillion in revenue employing 9 million people, according to American Express OPEN 2016 State of Women-owned Businesses.

We've come a long way. But, we dramatically lag men in the size of our businesses. A typical women-owned business generates one-fifth the revenue of its male counterpart. Women-owned businesses account for only 8% of employment while men account for 35%. However — importantly — employment in women-owned businesses is on the upswing: up 18% since the recession, while employment in men-owned businesses has declined.

No surprise, there's a lot supporting the growth of women-owned businesses. In November, 2016, Dell's Entrepreneur-in-Residence, Elizabeth Gore, launched a campaign — #whatWEneedtosucceed — asking the incoming President and Congress to help women entrepreneurs grow their businesses. The campaign generated 4,206 social media posts, reaching more than 74 million people and generating at least 28 media stories.

For the good of the economy and job creation, let's close the gap between men- and women-owned businesses. Everyone has a role to play. From government to investors, from corporations to women entrepreneurs, concrete actions can improve women entrepreneurs' ability to get financing.

Ladies, learn the ABCs of financing, why?

Because Women start companies with 50% less capital than their male counterparts, according Access to Capital by High-Growth Women-Owned Businesses. The more ambitious the woman, the greater the funding gap. Research finds that undercapitalized companies generate less revenue, employ fewer people and are less profitable.

Over the past few years, new financing options have emerged. Women excel at rewards-based crowdfunding. Other options are not well known, such as Community Development Financial Institutions (CDFI), and are tailor-made for women entrepreneurs. But before you assume that these financing options are for you, do your homework.

Our options vary, based on how fast you want to grow, how much risk you can handle, your industry's size, the potential of your business idea, your ability and your financial wherewithal. A Woman's Resource for Starting and Financing a Business is useful not just for startups but ongoing concerns too.

"Over the past few years, we've seen a lot of legislation to kickstart getting entrepreneurs the capital they desperately need to start and grow businesses," said Amy Millman, president of Springboard Enterprises, an accelerator for women-led businesses seeking equity financing. "More is needed." New and young companies are the primary source of job creation in the American economy, according to The Importance of Young Firms for Economic Growth, a report by the Kauffman Foundation, which researches and advocates on behalf of entrepreneurship.

"The New Markets Tax Credit [NMTC] program is transformative in its ability to bring capital not already at the table to communities in need," said Catherine Berman, founder of CNote, which helps savers get a better ROI by investing in CDFIs. NMTC are provided by the federal government to incentivize individuals and corporations to invest in underserved communities. CDFIs are one way to do this.

For every federal dollar spent, $8 in private investment has been made. NMTC has also generated 750,000 jobs from 2003 to 2012. They are capped at $3.5 billion and will expire in 2019.

The uncertainty about the renewal of NMTC keeps some entrepreneurs from using it for their business models and increasing the pool of capital available from the private sector for underserved small businesses. Congress needs to make NMTCs permanent and raise the cap to $5 billion.

Phasing out preferential tax treatment for a fund's carried interest

Being mindful that President Trump stated he wanted to get rid of the preferential treatment for a fund's carried interest, one of his election standpoints, Trish Costello, suggests removing it in phases, allowing funds that invest in women-led companies to continue to benefit for 5 years. Costello is founder of Portfolia, a crowdfunding platform for accredited investors to invest in consumer products, and CEO emeritus of the Kauffman Fellows Program, a leadership training program for VCs.

Structure emerging manager programs so female-founded firms qualify

A growing number of local and state agency pension funds are developing emerging manager programs in which a portion of the money allocated to venture is invested in female-founded VCs who have a track record of success in other firms. The reality is that these programs still have hurdles, making it impossible for most female-founded funds to qualify, noted Trish Costello. More government agencies need to create emerging manager's programs and structure them so female-founded funds qualify.

WIPP recommends that the SBA's Small Business Investment Companies (SBIC) create an emerging managers program. SBICs are privately owned investment companies that can borrow money from the federal government to augment the funds of private investors for small businesses needing equity and debt financing.

More women need to ante up

Women currently control 51%, or $14 trillion, of personal wealth in the U.S. and are expected to control $22 trillion by 2020, according to Financial Concerns of Women, a report by BMO Wealth Institute.

More women need to ante up. For those women for whom angel investing is too risky, debt investment options, such as CNote are emerging. Interestingly, becoming an angel may lead to becoming a VC, suggests Alicia Robb, senior fellow at the Kauffman Foundation and founder of the Rising Tide Program.

The Proposal

Now that we have thoroughly immersed and hopefully engrossed you in the world of financial investment, because it is necessary, if you want to become a Millionaire-Made Entrepreneur, or wise about money. Let us simplify what this all means to you, as a woman with a passion, purpose, and need for a plan.

There is funding for all innovative, creative and marketable ideas. However, the key is to refine your business model based upon your target objectives and your customer, while concurrently ensuring that you are filling a gap in the market. As we have discussed this is one of our innate gifts as women.

Not unlike Firress' New Rich culture, Jessica and Wendy are vested in the high-tech entrepreneurship arena and have created an entrepreneurial incubator program for women-by-women to learn how to transition what is in their minds, into a viable good or service that is marketable; and that will create them the resources for their desired lifestyle. If you want to learn more visit us at ElitePerformanceAcademy.us

INTERMISSION

CHAPTER 4: Live, Love, Pray or Get Out of Your Own Way

The Power of Immunity to Criticism
– Dr. Maltz

You might have noticed we did a play on words from the title of the bestselling book Eat, Love. Pray by American author Elizabeth Gilbert. If you recall a motion picture adaptation of the book was released in 2010.

In this movie, which is the memoir of 32-year-old, Elizabeth Gilbert (played by Julia Roberts), she is portrayed as an educated, married, home owner that has successful career as a writer. She was, however, unhappy in her marriage and initiated a divorce. She then embarked on a rebound relationship that did not work out either, leaving her devastated and alone. After finalizing her difficult divorce, she spent the next year traveling the world. She spent four months in Italy, eating and enjoying life ("Eat"). She spent three months in India, finding her spirituality ("Pray"). She ended the year in Bali, Indonesia, looking for "balance" of the two and fell in love with a Brazilian businessman ("Love").

Through this movie, we extrapolated various themes that speak to the reasons why women do not get out of their own way in life and business.

First, we tend to not take the time to find out, who we are and what we need, prior to trying to find it in others.

Secondly, similar to Elizabeth, who after experiencing repeated failed relationships and less than expected elation from her initial travel adventure, fall into sadness, perhaps even dare we say it? Depression!

There are other subtle but insidious themes of women and body image and our need for relationship. One very awesome exception found in this movie title was that a woman was portrayed as adventurous. Which we are, or at least want to be.

The Art of Self-Love

Based on what we have shared thus far, it may be that you are realizing that we as a gender have a great deal of uniqueness to offer, but also that there is a great deal of work needed to change perceptions of women and it begins with our self.

As women, we have been conditioned to concern ourselves with the wellbeing of others first, sometimes unfortunately to our own detriment.

We are going to challenge you to now take some time to explore your feelings and beliefs about yourself. For some this may require a deep dive to get to your core, so that you can build up your self-efficacy and worth.

Think of your core, as enveloped in layers, like an onion. The outer layers may be rough, torn or even tattered from exposure to the elements. But when you begin self-work, each layer that you are willing to peel back reveals dimensions of yourself that bring wonder, joy, but sometimes also pain to the forefront.

We are going to guide you through initially the superficial layers that emanate your self-worth and esteem to others.

Generally, the concept of self-esteem as anchored by various researchers is a socially built emotion representing perceptions and feelings about various self-images and self-concepts based on the need for the aspiration of authentic and efficacious functioning, belonging and acceptance within one's social group, achievement and competence in contrast to other members of individuals' group (Bruno & Njoku, 2014).

Signs of low self-esteem include:

(a) Feeling incompetent,

(b) Worthless,

(c) Exaggerated perfectionism and unrealistic about our abilities,

(d) Being overwhelmed with fear and negative thoughts,

(e) Feeling unloved,

(f) Fear of change,

(g) Being unrealistic about goals,

(h) Constant need for validation and recognition; and

(i) Distorted view of self and others (Esmaeil et al., 2014).

Esteem Booster Strategies

We believe that it begins with Action--WORK (that four letter word we mentioned at the onset of this book). "Work is, above all, an activity through which an individual fit into the world, creates new relations, uses talents, learns and grows to develop identity and a sense of belonging" (Safura et al., 2014). In this context work refers to any activity of value to others, whether it is being a homemaker, banker, executive or entrepreneur.

Consider the opposite, a situation, when you remained complacent and isolated. Not using your time in any productive manner. Did the experience provide you with any positive benefit? Some might argue, "Yes, it did, not doing anything is heaven." But, we would predict that most would feel as we have in the past, lonely, anxious, fearful and worthless. The truth is that we are active beings by the very nature of our creation.

In biblical times, the creation of Eve, from Adam's rib, is a perfect example. Adam had all the creatures on earth within his domain, but still he was unhappy. It was not until God created woman, as Adam's companion to collaboratively govern His creation through relationship and co-laboring that both Adam and Eve found fulfillment.

Appraisal of an individual's self is in fact the self-esteem. This concept has some common features that include:

(a) Security,

(b) Belongingness,

(c) Identity,

(d) Worthiness,

(e) Respect; and

(f) Competence.

These elements are the fundamentals of the concept. The most famous work is of Maslow (1943) who includes self-esteem in his needs of hierarchy. Self-esteem is disposed towards capability and ability of an individual to manage with apprehension.

Numerous generalists and psychologists have posited that self-esteem is established by the collaboration of Worthiness and Competency. (Garrety, Badham, Morrigan, Rifkin & Zanko, 2003)

The Why - Boost Self-Love for Self and the Next Generation

Esteem is cultivated in early childhood through interactions with others and the world. Quickly a child begins to internalize value laden language from those most respected in their home and those in their social community. These schemas are then formulated into an opinion about self.

As a child matures, in pre-adolescence [and even sooner as research now shows] the comparison and self-value game begins. This is a difficult stage of development and today with increasing incidences of bullying [a monster of an issue with the advent of virtual bullying], more and more children are growing up with very poor self-esteem.

Recent published research in January 2017 by the Science AAAH Journal advanced the conversation on how gender stereotypes about intellect emerge early and influence children's interests by age six.

In the study, it reveals that common stereotypes associate high-level intellectual ability (brilliance, genius, etc.) with men more than women. These stereotypes discourage women's pursuit of many prestigious careers; that is, women are underrepresented in fields whose members cherish brilliance (such as physics and philosophy). And this disparity can begin to emerge as young as at age six.

Sobering Facts About Girls & Self-Esteem

7 in 10 girls believe they are not good enough or do not measure up in some way, including their looks, performance in school and relationships with family and friends (Real Girls, Real Pressure: National Report on the State of Self-Esteem, Dove Self-Esteem Fund).

74% of girls say they are under pressure to please everyone (Girls Inc, The Supergirl Dilemma)

98%... of girls feel there is an immense pressure from external sources to look a certain way (National Report on Self Esteem)

92%... of teen girls would like to change something about the way they look, with body weight ranking the highest. (Dove campaign)

90%... of eating disorders are found in girls (National Association for Self Esteem)

1 in 4 girls today fall into various clinical diagnosis – depression, eating disorders, cutting, and other mental/emotional disorders. On top of these, many more report being constantly anxious, sleep deprived, and under significant pressure. (The Triple Bind, Steven Hinshaw)

By age thirteen, **53%** of American girls are "unhappy with their bodies." This grows to...**78%** by the time girls reach seventeen.

(National Institute on Media and the Family)

We have to change perceptions of women to support the next generation of women, and it begins with you.

If you desire to explore your perceived Self-Love and want to learn strategies that you can utilize to enhance your Self-Love take the few minute Fit-Life Score Assessment™ at: www.drjvera.com/fit-life-score-assessment/

We've got to tackle the Monster in the room

Before we can move on we have to address what Jessica, who is formally trained in psychology and applied human sciences, encounters regularly in practice; that beyond conscious mindset blocks there are deeper emotions at play, in some cases.

Jessica finds that women, more often than men, are challenged by depressive symptoms and comorbid anxiety. And that these emotions manifest as fears that block human potential.

In tackling the challenge to write about women, fear and business, Jessica and Wendy had to touch upon and validate this mammoth monster that can plague women and influence inner mindset - Depression.

Particularly since mood issues and more specifically major depression is the leading cause of disability and of years of productivity loss worldwide (according to World Health Organization). In addition, it is a significant contributing factor to the development and progression of systemic and organ diseases (Murray, Lopez, 1997).

If you have ever experienced a devastating life event or loss, then you may have lived through depressive symptoms of melancholy and anxiety, even in some cases perhaps symptoms of posttraumatic stress disorder.

Wendy recounts that for a time, during her catastrophic experience of being undermined by a colleague, she experienced memory lapses at work. This frightened her to no end, as one of Wendy's deep seeded fears is developing dementia or Alzheimer's. A disease that has been prevalent in her family. After she left the job, she recalls that there were days that she could not get out of bed, as she did not know what to do next.

Wendy's identity had become so wrapped up in her position at the hospital that to no longer be a viable member of the team, left her without immediate purpose. This experience made her question her efficacy as a leader, as well as her worthiness.

Another colleague of Wendy's, actually one of her past superiors experienced a similar incident (loss) when her leadership position that she had held for 20 plus years was eliminated without any warning. This once organizational executive leader, found herself feeling as though the, "Rug had been pulled out from under her feet." To this day, she continues to fight the emotions of panic and fear associated with loss of a job and the reality of having to transition and start again in middle age.

Wendy and her colleague's experiences are not unlike many women, who in comparison to men are more likely to report subjective distress and to suffer from anxiety and mood symptoms. Some Researchers have identified that, women may even have the "trait" of having more subjective distress in stressful situations compared to men. Studies have shown that even when men and women have equivalent physiological responses to the same stressful situation (no differences in heart rate or plasma cortisol), women self-report higher irritability and fear as well as decreased happiness compared to men (Kelly MM, Tyrka AR, Anderson GM, Price LH, Carpenter LL, 2007). Revealing that the subjective experience is more profoundly felt by women than man. No surprise here, as we are innately, emotionally intelligent.

Neuroscience also provides some explanation for the gender differences. Specific studies suggest a biological dysfunction in the emotion regulation centers of the brain underlying low affect, a symptom dimension common to both MDD and anxiety disorders in women (Seminowicz DA, Mayberg HS, McIntosh AR, Goldapple K, Kennedy S, Segal Z, Rafi-Tari S., 2004). Men secrete hormones (the main one being testosterone) that counterbalance their expression of anxiety symptoms, women do not.

Interestingly, for those of us who are not science geeks, the principle hormone affecting mood, is decreased somatostatin (a growth-inhibiting hormone and a marker for [GABA] neurons targeting cell observed in several brain regions in the corticolimbic network of mood regulation) Not to be confused with Serotonin (feel good hormone).

Because although Serotonin has an effect on mood and social behavior, appetite and digestion, sleep, memory and sexual desire and function as it relates to depression, it has yet to be confirmed whether decreased levels of serotonin contribute to depression or depression causes a decrease in serotonin levels. Albeit, it has been agreed that Serotonin is the FEEL-GOOD HORMONE therefore we want more of it.

4 Natural Ways to Increase Serotonin

• **Mood induction**: alterations in thought, either through psychotherapy or self-induction, could increase levels of serotonin if the interaction between serotonin synthesis and mood is a two-way relationship.

• **Light**: already used as a treatment for seasonal affective disorder, a few studies have suggested that it can be used to treat depression as well.

• **Exercise**: exercise has an antidepressant effect, and some research has suggested that it can increase brain serotonin function.

• **Diet**: foods that have higher levels of tryptophan (chickpeas) than others could be linked to improved mood and cognition, possibly due to increased serotonin levels.

Ladies drop-in and assess whether your mind blocks are situational or perhaps related to deeper issues that warrant care. In either case, knowing is important, then taking action is essential. Because even when an underlying mood issue is not inherent, we all grapple with our inner self-critic.

Your History of External versus Internal Messages about Self

Have you ever found that just when you've reached your perceived pinnacle objective, your negative inner voice became louder and louder? We have.

Jessica has been exploring this phenomenon for years. It baffles her, how it is that even when positive action is taken, that dreaded ruminating voice can continue. The solution, counterbalance it with positive affirmations.

Sounds easy, but in fact research supports the fact that negative inner self-talk is related to conscious and unconscious memories ingrained through linguistic programming. Simply stated, the things you heard said to you or about you and others during childhood stuck with you, particularly if they were encoded with charged emotions.

When Jessica was an adolescent, she was constantly described by her mother and others in her family based upon her outer appearance. In a Latin family comprised of trans-cultural experiences maintaining the feminine Latin women physique was paramount to the women of the clan. She often heard value statements such as, "She has such a pretty face, but why does she not take better care of herself (when Jessica was a little robust in body weight)" or after not seeing family for a while the commentary would go something like, "She must be doing well because look at her, she is slim and fit."

It was not until adulthood that Jessica realized that these remarks and her own body perceptions had led to several issues related to weight and eating issues. Jessica found that she could control this one area of her life, during stressful seasons, and she did. Today now a healthier weight, Jessica has learned to be very mindful of the words that she uses to describe her daughters to others and to themselves. A focus more so on health and wellbeing is the path that she has chosen to take. But she admits that it has to be a conscious effort, because it is very easy to fall back to value-laden language about ideal body types etc.

Negative language seems to be very penetrating of our psyche more so than positive affirming language. That is why research has found that when using positive affirmations, repetition is very necessary.

The truth is that our brains are prewired to retain negativity. The concept of negativity **bias** is not new. Early research led to theories such as The Prospect Theory, which evaluates the way people make choices when there is a known risk. So, negativity bias and the Prospect Theory advanced the idea that people are more likely to choose things based on their need to avoid negative experiences, rather than their desire to get positive experiences. (Roy F. Baumister, Ellen Tratslavsky, Kathleen Vohs, and Catrin Finkenauer). These psychologists concluded negative experiences or the **fear** of them has a greater impact on people than positive experiences.

The negative perspective is also found to be more contagious than the positive (Paul Rozin and Edward Royzman) and our attitudes are more heavily influenced by bad news than good news (John Cacioppo and his colleagues). Other researchers analyzed language to study negativity bias. For example, there are more negative emotional words (62 percent) than positive words (32 percent) in the English dictionary.

In our brains, there are two different systems for negative and positive stimuli. The amygdala uses approximately two thirds of its neurons to detect negative experiences, and once the brain starts looking for bad news, it is stored into long-term memory quickly.

Positive experiences have to be held in our awareness for more than 12 seconds in order for the transfer from short-term to long-term memory. Rick Hanson describes it in this way: "The brain is like Velcro for negative experiences but Teflon for positive ones."

There is some research that suggests that some people are just innately negative and have a difficult time putting a positive spin on difficult situations. Christopher Nass, a professor of communication at Stanford University and co-author of "The Man Who Lied to His Laptop: What Machines Teach Us About Human Relationships," argues that we tend to see people who say negative things as being smarter than those who are positive. Thus, we are more likely to give greater weight to criticism than praise.

Psychologist Mihaly Csikszentimihalyi contends that unless we are occupied with other thoughts, worrying is the brain's default position. This is why, he says, "we must constantly strive to escape such 'psychic entropy' by learning to control our consciousness and direct our attention to activities which provide 'flow', activities which give positive feedback and strengthen our sense of purpose and achievement."

The solution cultivates and intentionally uses affirming positive self-talk to counterbalance subtly emerging negative inner talk. Invest in a daily practice of positive affirmations repeated throughout the day to reprogram those neuropathways. You have that ability, but it must become a daily practice.

This has to be part of your self-care regiment ladies. There is no easy fix when it comes to your brain. However, promising research findings are supportive of the fact that mindfulness not only reduces stress, but it can serve to cultivate mindful language, eating habits etc.

The Power of Empowerment

Empowerment is a term widely used by academics, policy makers and development workers, which has made it vague and difficult to conceptualize. For our purposes, we are utilizing the term to refer to a shifting of power from intrinsic to motivation of others to promote them to act out their potential. In the process, we are offering strategies and tools that can be used to enhance one's efficacy in the process.

In psychology, empowerment is conceived as an intrinsic motivation mode in people. People need inner strength and desire to influence other people (Jay, Alan, Henkin & Duemer, 2003). Empowerment is rooted in motivational desires of people.

Any strategy which increases the person's determination and their self-sufficiency will lead to their empowerment. In fact, empowerment is the making of situations for improving the individuals' motivation in fulfilling their responsibilities through improving their self-esteem (Laschinger, Finegan, Shamian, & Wilk, 2004).

The most powerful influence one can have on another human being is based in authenticity and the resonance of shared experiences. Jessica explains that for the better part of her life, she had been riddled with the shame and guilt that she harbored unbeknownst to her in unconscious mind from childhood sexual abuse. Yet, others, who have told her that she was their mentor early on in their careers, stated that she was perceived as a feisty, powerful young adult, with very strong convictions and protective capacities. Jessica assumed that they were gifts of learning to do business.

However, a night would arrive, when Jessica would find that her response to a situation would be so out of proportion that it warranted exploration. Baffled by the experience Jessica started to explore her feelings and memories to pinpoint the cause for her bizarre over reaction. She started self-work, as she had always traditionally done and it started to resurface, trauma memories, at least the superficial ones that were not deeply internalized. The connections were made, and although there was the realization of why and what had happened, Jessica still did not fully appreciate the impact of these trauma memories on her conscious mind and behavior.

She later learned why it was that her inner voice became so over baring and consuming, at a time in her life, when seemingly everything was going 'right'.

During this time, she did not have a mentor. But being the inquisitive person that she is, she started learning all she could about the brain. In her case, she leaned into knowledge not the boardroom, and made a discovery. She found out what it means to have a brain on fire, or toxic brain, as it is referred to in the literature today.

Why is this important, because when we are in relationship with others, which as we have established women need, it may one day become important to know why a person responds the way they do. Particularly when you are in a position to empower that person through a difficult situation.

Many have written about the toxic brain, but simply explained it is when the person remains in a state of heightened alertness, like in the phenomenon of 'flight or fight mode'. However, in the case of a toxic brain, this reaction does not turn off, when the perceived danger is no longer present.

This phenomenon is very prevalent among individuals who have lived through multiple childhood adverse experiences. A study completed by Kaiser Permanente from 1995 to 1997 initially concluded that multiple adverse negative experiences in early childhood has a tremendous impact on future violence, victimization, and perpetration, as well as lifelong health and opportunity. As such, early experiences were identified as an important public health issue.

The ACE Study utilized data from over 17,000 Health Maintenance Organization members from Southern California receiving physical exams completed confidential surveys regarding their childhood experiences and current health status and behaviors. This longitudinal study found that if a person has had three or four adverse childhood experiences the compounding stress of this on the developing child's mind has long term health implications.

The CDC continues ongoing surveillance of ACEs by assessing the medical status of the study participants via periodic updates of morbidity and mortality data to this day.

The findings of this groundbreaking study between the CDC and mental health community has far reaching implication for the individual and our society. First, if you have suffered childhood adverse experiences then self-care and in some cases seeking professional care is paramount to your physical health and lifespan.

Secondly, it provides us with further knowledge to consider when in relationship with others. Some may not be quick to disclose their histories, or even been fully aware of it, but when we engage in a trusting relationship it provides us with a further dimension for sensitivity and to cultivate compassion.

Through the study of mindfulness practices, Jessica learned to master stress reduction for herself and has taught and mentored others in the practice, so that they too can live healthier and longer lives. In essence, through her mindfulness instructor, she was empowered to find a way of being, in the moment. Keep in mind that the practice is lifelong.

Being present, not reacting, but responding intentionally to situations, being cognizant of underlying operating thoughts, but not engaging one's critical mind, rather allowing the thoughts to flow in and out and purposing to focus attention on being. These were the skills imparted by her mentor and guide, Sharon Theroux, Ph.D.

Sharon's teacher, Jon Kabat-Zinn impresses, "The only time you ever have in which to learn anything or see anything or feel anything, or express any feeling or emotion, or respond to an event, or grow, or heal, is this moment, because this is the only moment any of us ever gets. You're only here now; you're only alive in this moment."

That is why we value the gift of being and being able to empower others. Some researchers posit that it is based upon our determinant need to influence and control, but we offer another perspective, based upon our need to uplift and to transform the sociocultural perspective of women in our society. Not at the cost of under-valuing our counterpart, men, but rather for the purpose of bringing attention to the lost presumptive that collectively men and women leveraging different skills, talents, and gifts more can be accomplished for the good of all.

Empowering is a means to equip one another with strategies and tools that might not be in our repertoire in the moment, but that through collaboration with our sisters, can become.

An aside caveat, although we only superficially touched upon the influences of the subconscious mind, it is imperative that even, if one has not experienced ACEs, there is a need to explore stressors and precipitants that lead to reactive manifestations that impact self-esteem and performance.

To take the point home, Jessica shares that when she was at the height of her business success in her twenties, there was this nagging underlying voice that constantly was in her ear saying, "You are not good enough. You don't deserve this." To her dismay, the voice overpowered her skills, talents, resources, everything, and it led to self-sabotage.

Jessica learned first-hand what can happen when you do not get out of your own way. She was so consumed with these negative thoughts and emotions, that she stopped being creative, innovative, and intuitive. Instead she operated out of fear, having panic attacks, worrying about things that were not even reality such as not getting paid on receivables, letting everyone down, and thinking that her only worth was associated with her outward appearance. She thought, "I'm a fraud."

Because she didn't get out of her own way, seek alternative leadership [at the time for her companies], since she was not up for the task, she ended up selling parts of her corporate stock privately, stock piled resources and set out on a new course. Today when she looks back, she regrets not having done things a little differently. But, then she is reminded that the inherence from her entrepreneurial ventures served to finance her life till today. Everything has its season!

Now that Jessica's daughters are almost grown and Wendy is once again in Florida, the ladies have rekindled their collaborative efforts, but this time with a higher purpose, as they are cofounders of Elite Foundation, a nonprofit devoted to the freedom of children and women enslaved and trafficked worldwide. They share a passion to empower, teach, and to mentor all women through their pain to experience freedom to flourish in entrepreneurship.

Elite Foundation offers joint venture opportunities and licenses products to help women create income for their households. Their moonshot is to save 1,000,000 women and children from modern day slavery, by 2040, by funding grass root providers and organizations that rescue, rehabilitate and reintegrate victims to experience the fullness of their life.

CHAPTER 5: The Sisterhood of the Traveling Pants that Fit Us All

**Giving connects two people, the giver and the receiver,
and this connection gives birth to a new sense of belonging.
– Deepak Chopra**

Ann Brashares novels inspired a series of movies that followed four young girls into adulthood during crucial life experience. They succeed due to their loyal support of each other, symbolized by a pair of jeans (the "Travelling Pants") that they take turns wearing and that fits all of their body types perfectly. Each of the four main female friends are different. Shy Lena, the traditionalist's character is rooted in European family drama that takes her to a picturesque Greek island. She falls in love with a sensitive boy in spite of the families' old-fashioned feud. She learns to assert herself and finally wins the family's permission to date the young man, but over the course of the sequels Shy's relationship falters, she returns to college to complete her education, finds another relationship, and then her old love comes back to reclaim what they had.

Brash Bridget, the athletic, beautiful blond, starts off getting involved with an older man, the relationship goes nowhere, but she loses her virtue. Her storyline follows reconnection with her grandmother after many years, adventures in archeology and finding ancestral roots, as well as coming to terms with the fact that her mother's suicide [secondary to mental illness] was not her fault.

Tibby, the existentialist sour-tempered one, experiences loss, uses expressive art to reconcile the dissonance of her experience, falls in love, thinks she is pregnant; and lives through what can happen when an unplanned pregnancy arrives. Ultimately Tibby finds her life-partner, who was the young man she had dated all along, but had pushed away out of fear of rejection.

Carmen, an emotional Latin girl with low self-esteem, deals with the challenges of being a child of divorced parents, and of pursuing her dreams from an underdog position, in an elitist artistic environment. Carmen falls in love, becomes a big sister, and gains her self-worth, and identity through her love of self and her sisterhood.

This movie trilogy offered rich thematic content related to the power of developing close friendships, a sisterhood; predicated upon the crucial skill of networking and tribe building. As well, it clearly portrayed how, seemingly different women can find points of connection to empower, uplift, and promote one another. And that doing so benefits the tribe as a whole. Underlying themes of love, trust, gratitude, empathy, and how we women can be catty and hard on one another is also depicted.

What Size Pants Do You Wear?

Many of us, who have grown up in the 20th century have heard language such as, take care of your appearance, learn what you can, [maybe] go out and get a job to help with the finances or make sure you find a good man. Our beliefs about our roles as women, money, and relationship were linguistically ingrained in us since childhood.

When Jessica and Wendy grew up they had very different experiences around who they needed to become as women, about money, and relationship. Both were raised in atypical types of family systems.

Jessica primarily was raised by a single parent, (by her mother) within a blended system with four brothers. Wendy was raised by her grandparents, who adopted her after her biological mother could no longer adequately parent her. She was raised in a blended family where her older siblings, who were actually biologically her uncles and aunts, had left the home already and her biological half brothers and sisters lived elsewhere, but did visit often while younger. Wendy remembers that her bio-siblings were more like cousins to her at that time.   Wendy's grandfather passed away when Wendy was 7, leaving her grandmother to raise Wendy alone.

Each had a strong-female role model in the home, who nurtured and loved them. Wendy's parents worked hard, raised her as an only child for most of her childhood, and gave her access to everything that that they could to meet her needs and wants.

In contrast, Jessica lived in what might be considered almost poverty, growing up in government subsidized housing, and moving residences over 20 times before completing high school. Because her single parent could not afford the increasing rent. Jessica worked from a young age, 14, earning her own money to help in the household, by not being a complete financial burden.

Also, although Wendy had her education paid for her through her first master's degree, when she was given the opportunity for admission into medical school, she turned it down, because she did not want her mother paying from her savings. Wendy recalls, "My parents saved every penny and put money away for me since I was born. They were raised in the Great Depression, so I guess they were worried about ensuring that they or I never went without. Also, because my brothers and sisters, who had their own families were not in the house anymore, but still could see how my parents spoiled me, there was some rivalry around money."

Jessica on the other hand worked her way through school, paying for it herself through various and multiple jobs. Jessica recalls of a time that she arrived at her orthodontist's office, she was about 16; and they would not treat her, because her mother had fallen behind in payments. The following appointment, Jessica showed-up and paid the balance all in coins and one dollar bills. The balance had been just under $1,500.00.

When Jessica became of adult age, she started university paying for it herself and with scholarships and grants; but when her mother became ill, she ventured into the world of entrepreneurism.

Know Your Money Story...Why?

In relationships, there is one sure facet of transaction that can ruin built trust and that is the misappropriation or use of resources (money). Keep in mind that since the beginning of man, there has always been a mode of trade with value.

2,700 years ago, the first coin money was invented in Turkey and the ancient Chinese invented the first paper currency. And from this point on our current currency economy was created.

Today, alternates to metal coins and paper bills are emerging. A new currency has emerged called Bitcoin. Bitcoin was created in 2009 by an unknown person using the alias Satoshi Nakamoto. Transactions are made with no middle men – meaning, no banks! There are no transaction fees and no need to give your real name. More merchants are accepting them more: You can buy webhosting services, pizza or even manicures using Bitcoin now.

Bitcoins can also be used to buy merchandise anonymously. In addition, international payments are easy and cheap because bitcoins are not tied to any country or subject to regulation. Small businesses may like Bitcoins because there are no credit card fees. Some people just buy bitcoins as an investment, hoping that they'll go up in value.

However, because Wendy and Jessica's hearts are stirred by their desire to eradicate human exploitation, the fastest growing criminal enterprise, the impact of Bitcoin has been a cause for concern. Criminals are utilizing it to foster online transactions to purchase children and women worldwide without the risk of being traced through their transaction.

Not to get off topic, but the reality is sobering when advancements in technology are used for evil, instead of to promote humanity. The point being that **money is an exchange value and nothing more**. There is no need to place any other value on it, except as it pertains to knowing that if you are accumulating wealth, **it is because you have given value to others.**

When we looked at the stats on the main reasons for divorce, finances are among the top three reasons. It's not usually the lack of finances that causes the divorce, but the lack of compatibility in the financial arena. The same issue can translate into the business arena. Women are typically perceived as resourceful and financially frugal. But this is not always the case.

Differences in beliefs about money, self, and relationship, although learned, can be reframed if they are actually creating mind blocks. From our upbringing, we revealed several different beliefs about money:

Wendy:

- It can buy what you want and need
- It's easy to get – accessible
- It's dispensable – replaceable
- There is never enough
- It gives me security

Jessica:

- It's evil – money is bad (reality money was created as an exchange medium for the value of traded goods. So, it is just an expression of value. If you have a lot of money that means that you have created a lot of value, for other people).

- It creates power differentials

- It can buy things but it doesn't buy love

- You work hard, you earn money.

- Passive income what is that?

Despite these differences, ever since Wendy and Jessica have been doing business together, they have never encountered financial issues. Jessica traditionally leaves the finances to Wendy, whom she has learned to trust.

After the market crash of 2008, both ladies experienced financial losses, therefore today they find that at times, they do have despairing views about spending. But as they are aware of this, they purpose to work through them.

Wendy's beliefs about money were challenged after the demise of her second marriage. It was the first time that she experienced the **Fear of Scarcity**. You see Wendy, thought she met the love of her life. But in reality, this man was incapable of true love and stripped her of every bit of resource she had accumulated both emotionally and financially. She recalls being in a bath, sobbing, and feeling totally scared, "Because for the first time in my life I had no money and nowhere to get it from to continue to pay my bills." Wendy had not only depleted all of her liquid assets to bail her then husband out of debt, but she had gotten into debt to build his practice, over and over again. The result, surmounting debt load that she continued to pay, even after her divorce was finalized. This was a new experience for Wendy, one that she has resigned, "Will not happen again." Wendy has since learned to set aside pride and to let go of the shame for getting into life's messes, and has moved forward in her life.

Jessica's principle struggle with beliefs about money arose from a disparity in earnings between herself and her spouse. It took them over a decade to work through their money issues. Today Jessica and her husband share the belief that they are stewards of resources; and that they have a responsibility to manage them effectively. Jessica and her husband have been debt-free for the last nine years and they are slowly rebuilding from their losses of 2008. However, an ongoing challenge is that Jessica's husband remains in a scarcity mindset; whereas Jessica believes that there is no fear in gaining abundance through calculated risk and hard work.

Maggie Baker, Ph.D. identifies the myths about the relationship between beliefs about money and behavior with money and the incongruence that all too often exists. She and others point out that, although knowing your beliefs about money is important, it is not until you closely examine your behavior with money that you are able to further refine your beliefs to align with money behavior.

Wendy admits that she had never learned to save, like her parents always did, and her experience of losing what she had managed to put away for her retirement, left her with a sense of despair, for a time. Albeit, when she explored her spending habits, Wendy realized that she now employs discretion and is mindful about where she divests her assets more so than any other time in her life. Wendy stated, "It was a hard lesson to learn, but I am better off for it. I now appreciate that it is not money that is the issue, but rather all the backstory that goes with it that I have to take the time to learn about before investing in another relationship that is not going to be equally supported." Today, Wendy is savvier about saving, investments, and takes advantage of financial counseling.

Jessica having explored her household spending for over the last 10 years has been able to identify that she actually likes managing numbers (go figure, as she admits she never liked math) and that she is able to identify patterns in their spending behavior that speaks volumes about changes in her marital relationship. For example, for a season, Jessica's husband remained home with their first child, in her infancy. Jessica became the primary earner and although she preferred it this way, the reversal of traditional roles actually led to some discord in their relationship. Both were happier with the division of their household labor, but Jessica realized that she was actually devaluing her husband because he was not earning money at the time.

Funny right, the desired outcome that Jessica sought at the time, to be able to return to work, as she was not finding efficacy in being home, became the root cause that led her to disrespect her husband. Although they worked through this, it became a life lesson in respect, communication and being very clear about what each person needs and wants in their relationship with one another.

Also, Jessica learned the principles of saving and investing, two skills at the time believed to be luxuries.

Based upon their different experiences with money and their learned associated behaviors, Jessica and Wendy have had to, at times, intentionally meet each other in the middle, particularly when it has pertained to spending, as an investment.

The key to their success has been that they do not take their eyes off the mark, their collaborative end game, to fund freedom of enslaved women and children through their nonprofit, by equipping all women to work through their pain to experience freedom to flourish in entrepreneurship.

How Much Money Do You Have In Your Back Pocket?

Can we think and grow rich? Napoleon Hill's book "Think and Grow Rich," published in 1937, started a revolutionary metaphilosophically grounded school of thought that was predicated upon the examination of a group of successful entrepreneurs [all men] of the time and their shared beliefs about wealth building.

Hill's original work served to influence and impact thinking about how one can manifest wealth in one's life. Emotions were posited to fuel and to attract by innate internal conditions that which one focused on. And that the opposite also held true that there are negatively charged emotions that repel.

Hill reported belief that desire, faith, visualization, auto-suggestion, and imagination are pre-requisites and that when combined with a plan, collaboration with the right minds, and focus of the subconscious mind everything is possible.

He emphasizes that intuition is a gift. One that we have explained is inherently disproportionally found in women more so than men. But Hill warns of the emotions of fear and the detrimental impact that they can have if, not well understood and dissipated. In particular, he states that, "Faith and fear make poor bedfellows. Where one is found the other cannot exist" (pg. 185).

Hill proposes that there are six basic fears (poverty, criticism, ill health, loss of love of someone, old age and death) that are universal; and that fear of criticism and ill health are the ones most worried about.

These and other similar early writings, were in many ways repositioned in the phenomenon of the emergence of the Law of Attraction. For those who might not be aware of what the Law of Attraction (LOA) is, it is the belief that the universe creates and provides for you that which your thoughts are focused on (similar to Hills' writing). Many believe it to be a universal law by which

"**Like Always Attracts Like**." The results of positive thoughts are always positive consequences. The same holds true for negative thoughts always leading to bad outcomes.

The beliefs held by the Law of Attraction were challenged by Neil Farber, M.D., Ph.D., C.L.C., C.P.T. who has written in a series of articles summarizing his findings of the efficacy of LOA. stating that," After reading every book from the originators of the law in the late 1800s and becoming a certified Advanced Practitioner of the Law of Attraction, by one of the authors of 'The Secret' [he concluded that there] is no validity to the school of thought and further that it actually can result in complacency and harm.

Dr. Farber further concluded that belief in the Law of Attraction is not a healthy concept; and pointed out the wrongs with the Law of Attraction that included: no scientific basis and that rather evidence is all anecdotal and creates a placebo effect. Furthermore, it is counterintuitive as the LOA promotes less motivation, energy, and success, poorer relationships, no planning, or action, support or compassion. It blames the victim and promotes mindlessness. To read more on Dr. Farber's work, click here

Our belief is that there is no need to throw the baby out with the bathwater. Although there is some value in employing positive visualization and even putting out positive emotion, to sit complacently waiting for the universe to somehow materialize all your heart's desires, that to us seems a lot like the fairytales we were told as young girls.

It is not to suggest that one not employ faith and belief in something greater than oneself, but the part about remaining complacent is what stumps us. We have never been that way, both Jessica and Wendy have always worked, and worked hard to achieve whatever goals they've set for themselves.

Yes of course, there have been those experiences when opportunities, doors have opened, without any action on our part. We call those blessings. But, if we did not take action to make the most of these opportunities then they would just go by, or perhaps they would not even be acknowledged, as what they are gifts from God.

The point is that having a positive disposition, putting faith in something bigger than yourself, taking life each day as an opportunity to do something with it, living in the moment, in gratitude, does not ensure that bad things won't happen.

We believe that is the difference between the Law of Attraction and the 'Law of Reality'. Life has ebbs and flows and maturity dictates that through experiences we learn, in most cases, things about ourselves, others, and the world in order to navigate through the next day a little better equipped and prepared. However, there are devastating challenges that no one is ever prepared for, in those instances, having your sisterhood is priceless.

The Feminine-View of the Law of Attraction

Sharon Lechter, revisited Hill's best seller book [with permission from the original author's legacy foundation], and repositioned the principle as she proposed it pertained to women. After reading her work and many others', it is fascinating to find that most authors agree on the unique characteristics of women to conceptualize resources (money) and relationship in very similar ways.

In contrast to Hill's work, Lechter proposed a practice roadmap for women, who have a burning desire, and recognized that it is the starting point of all achievement. However, she makes specific distinctions between wants and needs, where women draw their force, specifically from personal values, and how this influences decision-making.

According to Lechter one's money story can be rewritten, by taking six steps to turn desire for wealth into reality. Specifically, Lechter emphases that we have to be clear about one's goal, specifying committed action steps with a defined target date to achieve it. Recognition that there is no reality in something for nothing. She is quoted as stating, "A goal without a plan is simply a wish without burning desire." Emphasis is also placed upon defining one's mission, a mantra, through a clear and concise statement, that is visible and repeated multiple times daily.

Similar with many scholars, who have studied behaviors related to money, the key is to become money conscious and to dispel self-limiting and faulty beliefs about money. After all, it is not money itself that is the problem. Rather it is the value beliefs that you have given it and continue to give it that can become problematic.

Jessica and Wendy are resigned to view money (resources) as a means to an end. Surely it is not a mistake to admit that we all need resources for our daily living, and that we are willing to work to ensure that these needs are met. However, when we considered abundance of resources, typically this is an entirely different story.

Through experience, Jessica has observed that people sometimes have lost their integrity in pursuit of money. In addition to relationships and so much more. Money cannot be the sole reason for any activity.

That is why, Jessica and Wendy have purposed to have access to the resources that they need and want for themselves and their family members in their back pockets. And to seek to create abundance of resource through strategic plans that serve others. Their calling is of higher vibration (importance) than the insignificance of any material things that money could buy them.

After all it is relative, nothing of what we have accumulated on this earth will be taken with us, when our days of living are done. Its legacy work that is of greater value to the ladies.

Now to the business of creating a community of like-minded hearted women who share their values and beliefs. Women have an innate ability to foster and nurture trust, and as a result to build community.

The 'YaYa Sisterhood' [with a few honorary Dude members]

Similar to what was portrayed in the movie, women come in all shapes and sizes and from all walks of life. Each of us has uniqueness and assets that when refined and identified, serve to provide us with our own platform, but also with the means to promote our sisters in relationships.

What do you believe is your greatest asset?

What sets you apart from the other billions of souls on this planet?

These are questions of SIGNIFICANCE.

The answer is found in the examination of 'that within'. Each of us, no matter our genetic origin, cannot be replicated. Not even identical twins are genetically identical.

That within, is your ESSENCE and without it, you would not exist.

Since the turn of the century we have identified "aw-ha" phenomena that we have been unable to empirically substantiate and yet we know them to be real. Science has unlocked and explained some of the mysteries of how we physiologically function but there are still things that cannot be tested, touched, or consciously identified that make you who you are.

In former chapters, we trust that we provided findings from science that explain why women develop better expressive language skills, emotional intelligence, use intuitive and pragmatic problem-solving, and are master taskers. Generally speaking, these skills we have in common.

However, now in shifting our conversation to you, as an individual, our conversation has to also include phenomenon that are not scientifically prove-able.

Wendy and Jessica's faith is rooted in their common belief of God. The first writings of God, the Creator of our universe, emerged in the middle Ages, and the Bible has been the number one bestseller book - for the written Word throughout the last 2,000+ years. Therefore, even by human standards, the Bible is a fantastic reference book, even if you do not share their faith belief.

Within its pages, you will find parable after parable emphasizing that God created each of us with a preordained purpose in mind, and that His crafting of us does not end until His purpose is complete (Phil. 1:6 Jessica's Life Verse). Further, that each of us with integrity and love has a responsibility to sharpen (refine) each other for the good of the other. (Proverbs 27:17)

Whether you share our faith beliefs or not, these two pieces of information in and of themselves are pretty pragmatic. Each of us has a purpose in life and collectively we have a responsibility to bring out the best in each other. This may not always be the case at all times; but from our experience, even when we've been hard on each other, it has always been in love, and because we want the best for the other. We are YaYa sisters!

In the last decade, an increased interest and awareness of the significance of the mind-body-soul connection has emerged and led to more acceptance of what we as women have practiced since birth. An integrated model of being, rather than just recognizing and valuing what is found from our shoulders up.

Women have the gift of keen intuition, the ability to actively listen not only with one's ears, but all senses and to observe the whole person. The latter are skills that can also be cultivated over time. But the desire has to be intentional.

Let us explain further, get a group of women together and become a fly on the wall and just listen. We love to gab and we do it well. We express our emotions, when we find trust in another, and we share all of our experiences whether wins or losses. Women value each other's opinion and seek it, because we want a sounding board and in some cases advice.

The YaYa Sisterhood Rules of Engagement

The four lifelong friends in the movie, met in adolescence, therefore they grew-up together. How do you establish a level of trust when you just meet another person for the first time?

The answer is to use your God-given trait to nurture and to serve the person. When you lead with these traits, it fosters a foundation in respect and provides the building blocks for trust. However, relationships take time and effort. Therefore, be willing to give authentically, because BS can be spotted by everyone.

There are simple rules that we all should live by, whether you are a part of a sisterhood or not: (a) treat others the way you want to be treated; (b) build up, don't teardown; (c) be aware of your words; and (d) be present and add value.

Now you might be thinking, these ladies are writing from a utopic position. Where is this sisterhood, sign me up! Because reality according to the stats and our own personal experiences have proven that these rules are not customarily followed even among our inner circles.

We might be setting the bar high, but we don't believe so. We come from the perspective of the need for change. It has taken women over a hundred years to get the right to vote and it was only because of a movement that was led by women before us. Therefore, we have tremendous faith that when we come together we can make a difference. This does not mean 'us against them,' rather "us for us", instead of us against each other.

When Challenges Arise in the Ecosystem

Adversities in life are a given, therefore how do we uplift each other during those times in a meaningful way. Our position is that we all have to learn to turn our setbacks into our greatest set-ups for our next breakthrough.

Within a sisterhood there is a unique opportunity to see from the outside perspective what is not evident to the person, who is in the midst of the storm. Also, if we approach the situation from a value position, then solutions can be identified, even ones that might not want to be considered by the person at the time.

However, caution has to be given, that timing is a critical factor. It is typically prudent to 'test the waters of receptiveness,' if push-back ensues then do not lean in, at that moment, another opportunity will arise. In those situations, being present, a shoulder or ear, is what the person is actually seeking. She is not ready for the solution, but just wants to be heard.

The opportunity in the future, is sure to present itself, if you maintain the course and just keep showing up. This was the case with the four girls in the movie. Their lives took very different directions, but irrespective, each knew what the other needed and they took opportunities as they arose to be present for the other. It was this selfless giving of themselves that foster their sisterhood and led to the trustworthiness of their connections.

There are also those instances, when certain relationships are no longer purposeful. This might sound somewhat harsh, but we like to keep it real. There are those relationships that emerge in different seasons of one's life that are tolerated because of all the years known. However, you are aware that the relationship is toxic. What do you do in these instances?

It is important to cultivate discernment and it is our belief that this is accomplished through resilience. Resilience is one's ability to adapt despite significant life adversity. It is a phenomenon – a hypothetical construct that is inferred from your manifested competent functioning despite experiencing significant adversity. Resilience is a learned protective capacity. Therefore, experience dictates over time what benefits and what does not.

At the heart of resilience is belief in oneself and taking responsibility for oneself and one's choices. Therefore, through negative experience (more so than positive ones) you quickly learn that certain types of relationships benefit you and other's do not. However, it is easy to remain in a toxic relationship, when co-dependence is fostered. These types of relationships are more challenging to leave. There is also the matter of how vested you are in the relationship. But it can be done. It becomes a question of what is more important the wellbeing of both parties or the maintenance of an unhealthy relationship.

We have all experienced these types of relationships to some degree. Wendy recalls one relationship that was difficult for her to remove herself from. She had known this girlfriend since high school, but despite them maintaining sporadic contact through adulthood, their lives had gone in very different directions. Both had suffered their respective challenges, but Wendy felt that there was no reciprocity in the relationship. She often found herself bailing her friend out of the pit, but when she encountered a devastating blow in life, her girlfriend was nowhere to be found. Even after multiple attempts to rectify the relationship, Wendy felt it was time to move forward, knowing that she would be there if at all needed but that having that person in her life regularly was not healthy.

Jessica also shared a similar experience, and this is why, she learned early on that true friendship is precious. But also, that there are different types of friendships and that each should be valued.

When we examined what Facebook has accomplished through a virtual platform that was developed to enhance social connection, it is baffling how one can have thousands of 'so called' friends and yet, not be vested in their lives. We believe that the connections made on Facebook would be more accurately described as network contacts. Especially, since Facebook broadened its user-ship and offerings to align with media advertisement becoming one's friend may be more a part of a market networking campaign, rather than for simply social connection.

We are not suggesting that there is anything wrong with leveraging social media platforms to network, just that the rules of engagement be clearly defined, so as to avoid misunderstandings and conflict. Particularly in an era of proliferated social media freedom of speech and self-promotion.

The YaYa Sisterhood Circle of Influence

All of us can benefit from a big sister, that person, who can afford guidance when needed. Unfortunately, from all that we read, one of the areas that we as women in business tend to neglect, is mentorship of other up-and-coming women. Friendships are one type of relationship, we do well, because there is a mutual understanding of need for connection. However, in a mentoring relationship, there is some disparity of power and other reasons for the relationship outside of friendship.

Some of the most prominent women leaders in the world include Meg Whitman, Oprah Winfrey, Indra Nooyi, and Hillary Rodham Clinton. These are all very different women—from different backgrounds, with different education and careers spanning different industries. What they do have in common is the role that mentoring played in helping them along the way.

Mentoring is known to provide opportunities for protégés to gain a broader perspective and learn more about their business, as well as to network and build social capital (the value of connections to people and their networks).

Mentorship is especially important for women's success because they often have difficulty building social capital at work, particularly in settings where there are fewer women (Chrisler & McCreary, 2010). Since there is a growing body of evidence showing how a more gender-diversified C-suite impacts the bottom line (Boatman et al., 2011), this also makes mentorship an imperative for businesses.

Recent published literature in the arena of mentoring examined, "Are women proactive in seeking out mentors? Do women in more senior roles volunteer to mentor other women, or are they worried about boosting the competition? What will it take to make mentoring more commonplace?" The study of 318 women, from 19 different counties with a medium age of 48, revealed that women are still not seeking out mentorship and that they (those in mid-leadership) are not being asked to mentor. These results indicate a gap in development potential and dispel the typical stereotype that women in leadership are unwilling to mentor due to protectiveness of their authority.

Albeit, what was made evident is that men tend to seek and offer to mentor more readily, and women more typically need to be found and encouraged (Laff, 2009). It was postulated that the main reason women do not seek out mentorship, is due to fear of rejection. And the main reason women do not mentor other women is due to time.

A mentorship success story: Denise Morrison is a great example of how it pays to be proactive in seeking out mentors. Now the CEO of Campbell Soup Company, she credits early-career guidance from the right mentor with helping her achieve her current role (Emory, 2012). When she was director of sales planning at Nestlé in the 1980's, she began an informal mentorship with then CEO Alan MacDonald. She would go to MacDonald with questions, seek his advice, and share customer feedback insights. Before long, he had recommended her for a promotion which Morrison says was a defining moment in her career. She is now so dedicated to mentoring that she spends as much as 20 percent of her time advising and supporting others.

The 2013 article published by The Wall Street Journal featuring "The Tyranny of the Queen Bee" which depicts women who succeed in the workplace as so protective of their authority that they actively work to keep other women from assuming their place, serves to proliferate the stereotype that deters mentoring.

With the surmounting literature that speaks to the benefits to mentoring, how can we encourage or promote more of it? First, we have to increase the percentage of women in the upper echelon of organizations in leadership roles; and secondly, we have to advocate for more formal mentoring programs in organizations.

Lastly, we have to breakthrough stereotypes, take a risk, find someone, who you feel has the experience that you need to benefit from and then ASK. The worst thing that can happen is that the person tells you is "No."

Also, do not negate the fact that there are also younger women, adolescents and girls that need you to consider mentoring them. Not only does that booster your self-efficacy, but it serves to promote esteem in your protégé.

The lives of the four women in the sisterhood of the traveling pants, all found their individual purpose and they were able to co-exist, leverage each other strengths, and to meet each other's needs, as they arose, together!

CHAPTER 6: Change Lives Beginning with Your Own

The moment we believe that success is determined by an ingrained level of ability as opposed to resilience and hard work, we will be brittle in the face of adversity.

– Joshua Waitzkin

In this 2000 surprise breakout role, Erin Brockovich played by Julia Roberts, is depicted as a desperate for work, unskilled, single parent of three, who takes a relatively inconsequential job as a legal assistant in a California law firm for low wages. While organizing some paperwork pertaining to real estate cases, she is puzzled when she notices medical records in one of the files. On a whim, she does a little investigating of her own, and comes to suspect that land purchased by Pacific Gas and Electric (PG&E) is the same land on which chromium contamination resulted from PG&E's environmentally irresponsible actions.

Examination of local water records and interviews with residents ill from exposure to poisonous chromium confirm Erin's suspicions, but pursuit of legal proceedings against PG&E would seem beyond the capabilities of the small law firm she works at. Still, Erin succeeds in making her boss, Ed Masry (Albert Finney), as passionate about the case as she is, and he takes it on. Both Ed and Erin must make great sacrifices in their lives, as the legal costs spread Ed very thin, and the round-the-clock work takes Erin out of touch with both her boyfriend and her kids.

Erin encounters challenges with her boyfriend and children, who resent her absence and do not understand what is taking her away from their family and home. She perseveres through; and in the end, Erin's special ability to bond with the victims of chromium contamination and their families and Ed's legal and administrative prowess are the key ingredients to making the case against PG&E. As a team, they manage to successfully lay the groundwork for the payment of legal damages by PG&E to those harmed.

Where Erin is today, two decades after Erin Brockovich instigated the largest direct-action lawsuit in history, the gutsy mother of three is still fighting for clean water. Her most recent crusade in Flint, Michigan, reached the national stage prompting former President Obama to declare a state of emergency and the state's governor to activate the National Guard. In a post on Michigan Live, Brockovich is credited with bringing the controversy to a 'fever pitch'—something few other outlets have highlighted... For a woman crucified by the media for a drunken boating accident, and attacked by a doctor who claims the original water contamination she found in Hinkley, California, didn't cause cancer (a theory that the Center for Public Integrity struck down), her day-to-day resilience seems nothing short of triumphant (Beast Daily published January 19, 2016).

The main theme found in this real women's life story is related to finding one's passion and transforming it into one's purpose. The most divine caveat that is communicated is that one's passion-purpose is not always what one would expect it to be. Erin has no legal background or formal education. She took a risk, jumped in with both feet, found a cause and it has fueled her life to this day.

The back story is that Erin has experienced failed relationships and is raising three children on her own. However, she is providing for them, and is still able to live out her passion-purpose for others.

What is one's Passion-Purpose?

Really, it's a play on words but the meanings of the two words when combined express exactly what is needed in order to flourish in life. Passion is an almost uncontrollable emotion and purpose the reason for which something is done or created or for which something exists (Webster). The combined meaning is what everyone strives to find in their lifetime.

The sad thing is that too many never do, because they either get caught up in the status quo, not believing that they can offer anything more, or fear of failure blocks potential.

Have you noticed that in all the stories whether fiction or nonfiction that we have highlighted in this book, the individuals had to press down sometimes deep within to go behind their veil to find answers.

And in most cases, true freedom to flourish arose from 'being cornered' and having no option, but to succeed. Sometimes this is what it takes. People reaching their limit—being stretched, not being able to live as they are, because they are uncomfortable or a situation arises that makes the situation unbearable.

What we believe is essential is to change one's perspective about these seemingly difficult situations, to one of opportunity. Everything that occurs in life has a purpose, whether you want to believe it or not. We are promised that in this lifetime we will experience adversity. However, how you walk through the fire and how you come out the other side is entirely up to you.

Para-moralities of Living

When we decide or life's needs decide that we step into a role outside the home, it can become all-consuming leaving very little time for anything else. In these seasons, there is really no space to consider one's passions, of course if given the op tion, we will choose a vocational that aligns with our interests. But more times than not, we will accept positions based upon pay.

Once you start in a position, it is like you're on a roller-coaster and parts of the ride are enjoyable, but others, make your stomach drop, and you experience a hollowness in your gut. That discomfort can either motivate you to do something to eliminate it, or you just stick it out until the ride comes to an end.

But when faced with situations in life that warrant action, these are the moments when we have found that nuggets of gold can be dug up. For example, had Jessica's mother never fallen ill and unable to work, would she have had the entrepreneurial experience she did that put her on her current path? Or if Wendy had been left to grow up with her biological mother, and not adopted by her parents, would she be the executive professional she is today? In both cases the answer is No.

Neither women, if left to find their own path during that stage of their lives could say with great certainty that they would be where they are now. Even though the circumstances of their lives at the time were not favorable, just like Erin's in the movie, the sequence of events led them to opportunities they might not have had otherwise.

In Wendy's life, some of her greatest past fears, i.e. loss, developing Alzheimer's and being alone served to ignite her passion to pursue scientific study, entrepreneurship and activism. Similarly, Jessica's fear of not being good enough, fueled her passion to seek degree after degree and to equip herself to teach others, because she is a life-learner and knows that education is the root of prevention of exploitation.

Similarly, when you find yourself in pensive thought, during those sometimes-stolen moments, reflect and find the golden nuggets in those seemingly negative experiences. What you might identify as a passion-point might surprise you. We are not suggesting that you seek to pursue every passion, but if you do not love what you do, then it is work. Because the contrary also holds true.

Jessica can count on her fingers the days she has spent in her life working. The majority of her time, she reflects in gratitude, has been spent learning, creating, developing, and implementing passion-purpose assets for her legacy. Which to her is not work at all. It's a privilege.

Ladies your breakthrough opportunity is there for you to discover it. We would like to share an exercise that has helped thousands find that special something that ignites their soul and evolves into a passion-purpose to impact others.

It is that last ingredient, did you catch it, if your motivation is only to create resources and does not impact others; then, there is a missing element. We trust that you appreciate that we are all interconnected. You can attempt to exist in a vacuum, but that existence is no life at all. The essence that is you, was created from others, for you, and others.

It is a fundamental principle that we as humans are finally starting to grasp. Ironically the circuitry of a computer, an inanimate object that models our human brain in many ways, is the most precise metaphor we could use. The interconnectedness of the wiring and coding sequences have to integrate just right in order for the outward functioning of the object to operate.

Jessica has worked endless hours with at-risk adolescents, who are hell-bent on throwing away their lives to drugs and other senseless activities. She remarks, "Some of our children today are growing up either with a sense of entitlement, that everything can be acquired with minimal input or hopeless because they see no future worth pursuing for themselves." Her greatest sadness is predicated on a belief that we as a human race lose whatever potential invention, service, or any other advancement that could have been contributed by each of those children lost to a life of crime.

A similar truth is evident in literature that reveals that high percentages of girls are growing up without esteem and vision for themselves and their lives. Suicide rates are on the rise in North America. Researchers are examining all the comorbidity factors, but does it really matter the reality is that our kids are killing themselves before they even have a chance to find out what they could have been.

We have a responsibility to ourselves and to others to find our passion-purpose and to live it out, to impact the community. The next generation depends on it. Had Erin not pursued her found passion-purpose in activism for clean water, how many more lives would have been lost.

Here is the initial inner roadmap [exercise] mentioned:

The Seven (7) Essence Principles to Flourish

1) **E**xist – purpose

2) **S**oul – core-power

3) **S**ense – emotional intelligence

4) **E**manate – positivity

5) **N**avigate – ebbs and flows with resilience

6) **C**haracter – strength-building

7) **E**ssential – absolutes (GPS guiding principle system, know your beliefs, values and goals)

To access your free digital copy of the toolkit of strategies to work through each of these seven principle please go to: https://eliteperformanceacademy.us/the-big-secret/

When you master these seven core ESSENCE principles to Flourish, then – you will be well on your way to living your passion-purpose. Being on path, fortifies your ability to deflect outer negativity and it enhances self-worth.

However, when dissonance is allowed to continue, Self-Love is vulnerable and permeable. The influence of others' expectations, value judgements, and negative criticism become imprinted, and detrimentally affect your ability to achieve your desired goals. Under these conditions, Fear prevails and it results in inaction and stagnation. Leaving you feeling as though you are on the proverbial roller coaster ride again and again.

Wins are Nothing if They are not Shared

Erin and her partner, Ed Masry each brought different assets to the table. Neither alone would have been able to accomplish what they did together, win the largest direct-action lawsuit in history. Even though, Ed could have acted out of integrity and pushed Erin out of the deal, as she was 'just' a low paid paralegal in his small practice, he recognized her value to the case. Erin was the only person, whom the victims could resonated with, and this resulted in the victims' agreement to pursue the legal action in the first place.

The 5-C Principles of Successful Partnerships

There are **5 C's** that we have found are the principle ingredients to experience success in partnership. If there is no consensus on these, then the relationship is not likely to survive when the first signs of obstacle and resistance are encountered.

The first **C** is **Courage**. We believe that we have consensus that every human being on this planet has fears. If, a person tells you otherwise (which we remind you is a protective capacity) then they are either lying or suffering from a mental ailment. The latter is no joke, there are individuals who suffer from certain mental illnesses that disinhibit one's sense of danger and self-control. Thereby rendering them impulsive and with the tendency to seek out dangerous self-risk and harm behavior.

Courage speaks to the ability to walk through despite fear, in order to get to the desired outcome. In business, it could mean taking a risk, in order to get ahead, even when there is a significant possibility of loss. **Mark Zuckerberg** once told a group of young entrepreneurs at Y Combinator's Startup School in Palo Alto that it's risky not to take chances. "In a world that's changing really quickly, the only strategy that is guaranteed to fail is not taking risks," he said.

Vera Wang - Making a big career switch can be scary, but it can also be oh-so rewarding. When, as a young competitive figure skater, Vera Wang didn't make the 1968 U.S. Olympic team, she pursued a career in magazine editing. Then, when she didn't nab the spot for Vogue editor-in-chief, she went on to work as the design director for accessories at Ralph Lauren. Her newfound career in fashion (coupled with a dissatisfaction with the less-than-stylish dresses available when she was planning her own wedding) led to her ultimate pursuit of a career in bridal fashion design. And today? She's one of the biggest names in the business.

J. K. Rowling - It's hard to believe that publishing Harry Potter was ever considered to be a "risk," but J.K. Rowling's struggle to find someone who believed in the book as much as she did was a tough one. Even as a single mother living on welfare, though, Rowling wouldn't let any number of rejection letters stand in her way—she refused to stop believing in the work she had created. So, one year after landing an agent, she finally got the call: Harry Potter and the Philosopher's Stone was to be published by Bloomsbury Publishing in the London. The rest of Harry's (and Rowling's!) story is history!

Bill Gates - After two years at Harvard, a young Bill Gates took a risk that would end up giving way to the rest of his (wildly successful) career: He dropped out of college to found Microsoft. Today, Harvard's most successful dropout makes a point of urging students to stay in school ("getting a degree is a much surer path to success," he's said), but the idea behind his decision to drop out is still the same—sometimes, a great risk reaps great reward.

The **2ⁿᵈ C** is **Compassion**, which is a feeling of wanting to help someone who is sick, hungry, in trouble, etc. Wendy and Jessica believe that without compassion, which is clearly a component needed in relationship building and strategic business building alike; endeavors without it are directionless and do not foster a work culture that promotes employee retention.

Case in point; Peter Drucker used to say that all employees are volunteers, that business success was becoming more about the ability to attract top talent and then motivating that talent to do their absolute best work. The truth is employees do not leave jobs, they leave bosses.

This focus on relationships became an explicit goal at Juniper Network, where Scott Kreins spent 12 years as CEO and saw the company grow from a handful of enthusiastic engineers when we started to a company of 7,500 people and $4 billion in sales worldwide. The growth resulted from timing and good fortune to be delivering the right products, conceived at a time when the market needed them and central to growth was the ability for teams of people across the company to work together to achieve results that individually would not have been possible. Kreins reported, "the best way to develop a high-performance business for the long haul is to develop a caring, high-trust, relationship-centric culture. These cultures nurture a sense of purpose, of connection, and of compassion, where the business results we can measure are not the first priority of the enterprise, but rather a consequence enjoyed when leaders and teams practice the primary goal of building a caring community every day (By Project Compassion Business, May 2013).

The **3ʳᵈ C** is **Creativity** the use of imagination and original idea to produce something. This is essential to any enterprise, and as women we bring uniqueness in creativity that is not common place or commonly appreciated by men. Yet, women make up 80% of the consumer decision making in the world. Therefore, it would behoove businesses to start placing greater value on the creativity that a feminine perspective can bring to the drawing board when developing a service or product.

Creativity is often a key differentiator in the success of a company's individual departments and internal strategies, said Mike Mansbach, president of BlueJeans Network, a videoconferencing service.

"Not only does creative thinking produce ... winning sales and marketing campaigns that increase brand appeal to the end user, but [it] can also help foster a unique company culture that ultimately reflects and encourages creativity within each department," Mansbach told Business News Daily.

The **4**th **C** is **Collaboration** the ability to work together. The collaborative culture of an organization stems from its' shared beliefs, values, and business practices. Author and business consultant, Evan Rosen says collaboration is about creating value.

In Bloomberg Businessweek, Evan Rosen emphasizes every worker contributes knowledge to the business. Using an example at Dow Chemical, he writes, "The day's sales and inventory numbers are shared with everybody in the company, including the people doing the heaving lifting on the front lines. Dow acknowledges that people will do a better job when they know their actions contribute or detract from business results."

Former CEO of Campbell Soup, Doug Conant, is famous for handwritten notes to employees celebrating their contributions. Recognition through these and other high value communication practices further strengthens a collaborative culture, which leads to higher productivity, job satisfaction and employee retention

The **5**th **C** is **Commitment** the willingness to give your time and energy to something you believe in. Whether you're deeply invested in your career or starting a business, successful people commit to certain decisions that help shape them into, who they want to be professionally.

Wendy and Jessica recently met two exceptional people, who have impacted community for the last 30 years in very tangible significant ways that affect us all; through a successful partnership that was established in mutual admiration and respect.

Dr. Jolanda Janczewski (Chairman) and Mr. Dennis Lauchner (CEO) of CSS, Inc. met 30 years ago, through their shared occupational interest in safety and environmental health. Both grew up in very different social and economic environments, however they were intuitive enough to realize that they shared Courage, Compassion, Creativity and even a desire for Collaboration. What neither understood about the other initially was the level of Commitment each could deliver, particularly in the early years.

Per Mr. Lauchner, "Commitment is quite possibly the most difficult of the five C's, because it requires the most effort, literally. Throughout our relationship, Jolanda and I quickly learned that collaboration was essential to give life to creative business ideas that grew from our shared passion in the arena of the science of safety and health. We both were willing to risk our safety net of executive positions, demonstrating not only our individual courage, but our mutual trust in the fundamental vision for the start-up of a small business. However, without an equal commitment to survive the inevitable storms, making emotional and difficult decisions almost daily, putting in the long hours necessary to make the dream a reality; and never compromising our integrity by taking the easiest path...what we have built today would have never happened and we both knew that to give-up premature of achieving our goal was not an option for us or for those who were depending on us to succeed."

Today, CSS, Inc. is a thriving, diversified earth, space, and life sciences company that has tackled some of the most challenging environmental issues since 1988... from decontaminating the State Department's worldwide mail facility in Sterling, VA following the anthrax attacks shortly after 9/11... to the trenches of environmental challenges during Deep Water Horizon and Hurricane Katrina. CSS has designed and conducted experiments in microgravity, including research aboard the International Space Station, and processed scientific payloads for more than 60 NASA Space Transportation System missions. Both Dr. Janczewski and Mr. Lauchner remained fully committed to making their dreams a reality. And in their unique and pinnacle expression of Commitment, Jolanda and Dennis sold their business to the employees who helped them accomplish their dreams, by creating an ESOP in 2005.

In a recent discussion with Dr. Janczewski, she stated, "Finding one's passion is the key to true success, and should be more emphasized when we speak to aspiring professionals. In fact, I have been discussing the topic recently with our current CSS President about the "passionality" of our workforce. Our company is filled with wonderful, smart scientists, who are lucky to work in their chosen fields and are more passionate about their work than most. We have had an upfront look at the value it brings not only to the individual, but to the company as well, a win-win for all."

The story of Erin Brockovich as portrayed in the motion picture production, we believe is a perfect example of how one can find your passion-purpose in the least likely of places; and of having the courage, to step through the fire, and to raise one's hand for the good of others.

Passion ignites the soul and purpose directs the path!

SCENE II

CHAPTER 7: The Conundrum and Deservability of the Legally Blonde

> "Your beliefs become your thoughts. Your thoughts become your words. Your words become your actions. Your actions become your habits. Your habits become your values. Your values become your destiny."
>
> – Mahatma Gandhi

Legally Blonde inspired outrage initially [for blondes anyways]... in this pop culture classic, Reese Witherspoon plays Elle Woods, a ravishing Miss. Hawaiian Tropic, sorority president, and calendar girl, who is an immediate big hit on campus of her sun-drenched Los Angeles college. Elle is awarded admission into Law School on a whimsical effort to follow her perfect boyfriend, Warner Huntington III (Matthew Davis), a wealthy East Coast blue blood to college. The couple had been high school sweethearts. But in a turn of events, the plot leads down a windy road of betrayal and abandonment. You see, Elle's boyfriend fearing his snooty friends and family's reproach for his choice in girlfriends in college, a bubble-headed Elle, proceeds to dump Elle before heading off to graduate school at Harvard University.

Elle pines her loss, falling into seeming depression, spending days in isolation, but during a chance encounter while getting her nails done with her friends, she reads a newspaper story featuring Warner and his fiancé (a prim and proper prep school girl). In a plot to win back her old beau, Elle studies and is accepted to the same law school as Warner and his fiancé. Unfortunately, her plan does not turn out as anticipated as she becomes an object of scorn and ridicule, especially by Warner's fiancé. Despite her penchant for malls, makeup, and tanning, we find out that Elle is no dummy, and soon demonstrates her smarts to the elite Ivy League [portrayed] snobs through her poise, class, self-confident application of real world experience, courtroom victory, oh and of course fashion.

The Legally Blond series of movies follows the main character through her journey to finding Mr. Right, her passion for activism and leadership, all through a humorous genre. But the humor stops at the movie, because when we explore the stereotypical perceptions of women in society, we cannot negate the fact that jokes are made about the intelligence of a women based upon her appearance. Nor can we minimize the impact of our own contribution to the proliferation of these types of generalizations, by not showing up filled up, when the occasion warrants it.

Elle had the last laugh, as she buckled down, and was able to show-up in classes prepared. She found her passion-purpose and pursued it without excuse, and found her partner in life to support her and their life choices. Go Elle!

Tackling the Deservability Conundrum

Although, we're not all Caucasian, blonde, rich, and beautiful, Elle did offer up a few universal nuggets that we can carry with us. It's her determination and tenacity in the face of adversity that we love most (but only slightly more than her cute doggie Bruiser). Elle taught us to ignore the naysayers, work hard to achieve our goals, be yourself and to never let anyone tell you, you are not smart enough or you can't do it. Elle also boasts a powerful message about staying true to who you are and your strengths.

The mantra of, "You can do anything with a bit of hard work, commitment and persistence" resonates with Wendy and Jessica. Just like Elle, who set her sights on Harvard Law School, worked tirelessly to achieve her goal, studying around the clock and missing out on social events to excel on the LSAT, Wendy and Jessica believe you have to do the work.

If you're willing to make an effort, go the extra mile, there is no limit to what you can achieve.

However, all too often, we as women have a stumbling block, because we do not believe that we deserve success. According to Louise Hay author and one of the founders of the self-help movement, who coined the phrase 'Deservability', she posits that at the deepest core of our being we don't feel we deserve to have what we wish for and that this belief will block these things from coming into our lives. We end up settling for less than what we truly desire because of our own self-limiting belief.

The conundrum arises when there is confusion between what one desires and one's abilities to acquire and achieve it. And, further that when we do achieve something; we cannot accept credit for it, because we don't believe that we deserve it.

What a cyclical ride, make it stop.

We can't because there is more, in some cases, we do not even attempt or set-out to achieve something because we've bought into the lie that we cannot have it all. Wendy and Jessica both know that it is true to some extent that we cannot have it all at the same time; BUT we can have all that we want, when we chose to have it.

It all comes down to a choice. And this choice has far reaching implications because it impacts your ability to earn what you believe you are worth.

Early on in her career, Wendy recalls never being afraid to ask for what she wanted or what she thought she deserved, because of the influence of her parents, who instilled confidence and invested in her to gain the hard skills of her chosen vocation. However, due to Wendy's limited life skills, when she got her first pay check from her first employment experience and did not factor in tax deductions, she was struck by the reality of her net earnings. She immediately sought to rectify the situation. That's right, she walked into her superior's office and asked for more money.

Now we'd like to tell you that she got the raise, but she didn't. What Wendy did do, is she found a better paying job of course. Why, because she had the hard skills in her chosen vocation, and her sacrifice to get her degree had been substantial for her and her parents. Therefore, she knew that she was employable and her skills were in demand.

Throughout her career, Wendy has had both the experience of asking for what she thought she was worth and getting it, as well as the reverse experience. Her takeaway, in her current season of life, is that unfortunately, experience today is not always valued by others, that is why we have to be our own best advocates and show up to the table filled up and ready to over-deliver.

Jessica's experience through entrepreneur ventures gave her a different vantage view. In her case, she valued her worth, by engineering products and services that were value-added to her chosen industry and that provided her customers/clients with optimal return on their investment. What she recalls finding more difficult, then determining her own self-worth through monetary value was determining what to pay employees. Jessica had a tendency to over-value people and their potential and this did not serve her well in the beginning of her career.

She recalls of an experience in which she hired a young man, from within her companies' industry. This young man had tremendous promise. He was well versed in the business model and the needs of the industry. He bought a unique set of skills to the table. He was trained in indemnity insurance products and was very savvy. Over the course of a year this young man made great strides in the company and he was given a promotion into leadership.

However, this was Jessica's first life lesson in recognizing that not all individuals can lead. Over the proceeding few months after this young man's promotion, he began to engage in poor business practices (unbeknown to Jessica) and soon thereafter ended up before the authorities. It was later learned that this young man had been striking side-deals to boost his department's new client list numbers. Jessica realized that she had been rewarding him for the very behavior that led to his arrest and incarceration. Jessica's companies were not directly involved or affected by the litigation case that arose, however it was a significant lesson learned. Leadership can be learned, but it begins with the right core values.

John Maxwell and other self-development leadership coaches and mentors have provided a body of knowledge on leadership that posits that we all are able to cultivate leadership skills as part of our soft skills repertoire. And that by doing so our marketplace individual stock value naturally increases. No matter your role/position in life, everyone can be a leader in the community, among friends, family, peers etc. From this perspective leader create a vision, motivate, and inspire others to engage in the vision, manage the delivery of that vision and coach others so the vision can be achieved.

However, Maxwell contributed a phenomenon he termed, "The Law of the Lid" which refers to the lid that determines a person's level of effectiveness. Maxwell discusses that how successful we are going to be is determined by our ability to lead, that leadership is influence and our influence with people and therefore ability to lead develops through a process that evolves day by day. From this perspective wherever your leadership skills are at the moment is the lid of your business ability.

We know that we have not answered the conundrum dilemma but the best way to do so, is to begin from the beginning for the aspiring entrepreneur. Be patient, like Elle, you will be presently surprised by the outcome.

Intro to Entrepreneurship 101

Unfortunately, for most of us who have chosen a vocation out of the home, auto-education begins the day you set foot outside the comfort of your doorway. Until recently, there were no schools offering any type of formal training or education in entrepreneurship. In fact, if you wanted to learn about entrepreneurship, typically you would enroll in business administration classes or accounting. We might be dating ourselves LOL. Irrespective, the point is that the advent of formal training in entrepreneurship and high-tech entrepreneurship is still evolving today.

Remember the stats on entrepreneurship among women, we are the fastest growing segment in the economy. Sure, we have a long way to go to catch up to our gender counterpart, but more and more collaborative partnerships are being forged and small businesses are gaining recognition for their value to the overall economy of our country and globally.

Wendy pursued her Master's in Business Administration as a mature adult, when it was evident to her that in order to continue to forge up the corporate ladder, she needed to compete on at least an educational leveled field. Jessica has conferred a degree or specialization in every area of human applied science of interest to her. However, today one's efficacy is not always based upon the number of initials that follow our name. Rather, in our fast-evolving marketplace intuition, innovation, and strategic rethinking of how things have been done till now; and planning to fill a gap leveraging tech and automation is most valued and lucrative.

Even when you possess the hard skills in a vocation, taking the leap into entrepreneurship requires courage and added reliance on soft skill competencies. Why, because as an entrepreneur you typically wear many hats and initially (at least) have to do all of the operations and business development tasks yourself.

In the past most entrepreneurs, Jessica included had to 'wing it' build and learn as you go was the moto of the day. But the stats on failed new venture start-ups (97% in the first two years) speaks volumes to one of the main reasons we under took this endeavor to write this book.

In entrepreneurship, we have identified four core hard skills needed to get in the game and if you want to hack the fastest growing business segment, high-tech entrepreneurship;

4 Core Hard Skills

1. Finance,

2. Sales & Marketing,

3. Business Analytics and Logistics; and

4. Technology.

But it all starts with your well defined passion-purpose, to come to the table filled-up and ready to offer your unique selling proposition (USP).

Your Unique Golden Nugget Offering to the World

Your 3-Core Foundational Design Facet of Your USP

1. Dig and Define
       Know your Why

2. Excavate and Refine
       Know your What

3. Identify and Find
       Know your Who

The uniqueness of what you have to offer, can be found in the clues left from your past. Then once you identify it, explore why this is needed. Typically, it is because it offers a solution for a pain point. However, if your only motivation is money and not service, then you will fall short. Since we were created in community, it is implied that we all have something to offer another and vice versa.

Finding your special something is a process, but once you identify it, knowing your what, is answered. Then do what we do best, find the gap in the marketplace and fill it, in your own special way. However, do not neglect identifying your customer. The people with the pain point that you have the unique solution for. This can be accomplished in many ways, but you can start with a simple market analysis of her service or goods.

Most small business owners, start their venture on the basis of a passion alone. They do not give enough value to the complete process and then sometimes find that there isn't enough of a market share to support their dream. Back to the drawing board...but don't give up. Just maybe change course.

If All Else Fails Bend and Snap, Leverage Your Soft and Fluffy Skills

Soft skills, are the complement of innate strengths (a combination of interpersonal people skills, social skills, communication skills, character traits, attitudes, career attributes, social intelligence and emotional intelligence etc., you possess within. These skills can be utilized to foster relationships and cultivate your **USP**. The key, which we are going to provide is how to unlock and leverage them to serve others and in the process, yourself.

Wendy remembers her mother used to say, "You can't teach nice." Although that is true, we believe that one can learn to be nice, if you value interpersonal relationships and how you are perceived.

ARE soft and fluffy skills essential in today's marketplace?

Elle fashionably showed us, we do need soft skills, if we are going to use our technical skills and knowledge effectively and efficiently. In the world of tech, where you can have thousands of friends and followers, authentic connections are challenging. There is a whole new slew of applications that were created to keep you connected and visible among your tribe. You can snapchat, tweet, video live or stream, email, door mail, text mail etc.

Whatever means of communication you choose to maintain with your tribe, enhancing your soft and fluffy skills improves the means and quality of how we interact with others. They permit us to get the work done timely and to influence how we feel about what we do and how others perceive us and our work. Although traditionally it used to be our hard skills that got us in the door [they are still valued in brick & mortar endeavors]; today, greater emphasis is placed on soft skills because they keep us there and open up new windows, when needed.

Your Soft and Fluffy Toolkit

The Top 15 Soft Skills Needed to Thrive

1. **Communication** – oral, speaking capability, written, presenting, listening.

2. **Courtesy** – manners, etiquette, business etiquette, gracious, says please and thank you, respectful.

3. **Flexibility** – adaptability, willing to change, lifelong learner, accepts new things, adjusts, teachable.

4. **Change Management** - challenge with new skills, tasks, outside your comfort zone

5. **Integrity** – honest, ethical, high morals, has personal values, does what's right.

6. **Interpersonal skills** – nice, personable, sense of humor, friendly, nurturing, empathetic, has self-control, patience, sociability, warmth, social skills, temperament to manage adversity

7. **Drive, Ambition, and Stamina** - your engine to move things forward, hard work, loyalty, initiative, self-motivation, work ethic.

8. **Positive Attitude** – optimistic, enthusiastic, encouraging, happy, confident.

9. **Professionalism** – businesslike, well-dressed, appearance, poised.

10. **Responsibility** – accountable, reliable, gets the job done, resourceful, self-disciplined, wants to do well, conscientious, common sense.

11. **Teamwork** – cooperative, gets along with others, agreeable, supportive, helpful, and collaborative.

12. **Problem Solving and Critical Thinking**- using logic and experience to solve things

13. **Time Management**- prioritization, productivity

14. **Resilience**- tenacity, "Fake it till you make it", Chutzpah, guts

15. **Emotional Intelligence-Emotional Awareness** - ability to harness emotions and then apply them, apply them to tasks like thinking and problem solving, manage and regulate your own emotions

Elle's 11 Basic Life Lessons We'd Do Well to Heed

1. Women business owners need real life experience... You can rote-learn all the accounting and business language in the world but what's going to make you a superb business woman is your ability to use real life experience to help your clients and make great sales offerings.

As Elle pointed out in court, the cardinal rule of perm maintenance is that you're forbidden to wash your hair for 24 hours afterwards, a fact which secured a case-winning admission in cross examination. 'The rules of hair care are simple and finite. Any Cosmo girl would've known."

Elle used real life knowledge to cross-examine her witness and to discredit her testimony. And she taught as the 'bend and snap' to gain the attention of an admirer. All in a day's work.

So, whether it's that part time job you had in college, the crazy teacher you learned from in high school or what you've gleaned about food presentation from Facebook feeds what you know about life and people is just as, if not more, important as how you learn and apply the rules of your business. You never know when that tabloid magazine you read at the doctor's office or grocery line will spark your next big idea!

Also, we have to use our experience both good and bad in order to know what to do and when to do it. Our experience shapes us and guide us to know how to continue along our journey.

In her book Lean In, Sheryl Sandberg suggests that we set big goals and be ambitious about figuring it out. In other words, we "Fake it till we make it".

Also, we need others to feel they know us, and that they want to get to know us better. This will help us in most situations.

We need to connect to our prospects and customers/avatar. We have to get to know them, and their main pain points to offer solutions. But most important you have to be authentic and be willing to be transparent in order for others to resonate with your message.

2. It helps to think outside the box

Don't be a copycat and regurgitate tired old arguments that you think others want to hear. In **Legally Blonde**, When Warner Huntington III makes a comment about legal precedent during a law lecture, Elle takes the opportunity to use her own powers of deduction and forms her own logic, albeit a unique idea for the case being examined.

Logic and critical thinking are essential for higher executive functioning. It takes vision, seeing beyond the books and normal limits of your formal training as well as not being afraid to put your hand up in a conversation and ask questions. Not knowing an answer and seeking to get the answer is the process by which some of the greatest innovations were made.

Innovation in the quickly evolving high-tech and online business arena requires adopting the 'New Rich' mentality, if you are going to succeed, by gaining time, flexibility and mobility. Within this context scaling and automation are crucial [more on this in the next chapter].

You might be asking yourself why the metaphor of the box is so commonly used. Simple, because it conveys conformity. In past, employees were rewarded for adhering to operational systems, but now, being able to create your own box or better yet, erasing all dividing lines has greater value, as it fosters a culture of collaboration and leveraging against other knowledge not already contained.

Unfortunately, not all industries adhere to this paradigm shift in organizational psychology. Take for example the healthcare industry. Healthcare is behind in implementing and leveraging technology [in most cases], customer-centeredness and optimizing timely and cost-effective outcomes. Wendy has long advocated that healthcare providers would do well to explore other industries that could positively impact their operations.

3. Don't be afraid to stand out from the crowd

Why on earth would we want to be like everyone else?
Why would we want to conform to an industry stereotype?
Answer – Because it's safe!

What makes the world (and the profession) an interesting place is that we are all different – we all think and work differently (and thank goodness for that!).

So, it might sound like a cliché but don't lose yourself as you begin your business. If, like Elle, the color pink, shopping, shoes and scented paper are your thing, then don't be ashamed – embrace it! If your favorite thing to do on a weekend is to sit and watch The Real Housewives and eat jars of pickles in your undies, that's fine too.

Just because you like quirky or frivolous pant suits or snort when you laugh doesn't negate your intelligence or business skills and you don't have to be serious or two-dimensional. Find a way to combine what you love along with your business and above all keep it real.

Elle was laughed at during her first law lecture, humiliated in her bunny outfit, rejected by a study group and you know what? She never gave up and never lost her sense of self – she just became more determined to succeed.

Elle's graduation speech, highlights the point that you should always have faith in yourself. Don't try to change yourself to achieve success – just be you and be the best version of 'you' that you can be. You can be either your worst enemy or best friend. The only person standing between you and your goals is yourself.

Have you seen the video called "The lone nut" it is a very inspirational video that starts off with a shirtless man dancing, soon there is a second, and then more and more people join in, making complete fools out of themselves but they were now the norm and no longer "the lone nut?" They started a revolution to where now the individuals not dancing were the outcasts. This is a great example of how we can persist and stand out to be who we are and get others to follow.

Can you think of times where you purposefully stood out and didn't do what was expected? What were the results of that behavior? If positive, did it reinforce you to continue? If negative, did you give up or change?

4. Build your client's trust:

Despite criticism from Callahan and the rest of his team, Elle stayed true to her word and kept Brooke's potentially career-ending alibi confession a secret. Elle shows us how important it is to maintain integrity. It is vital to building trusting relationships. When trust is fostered, value is inherent, and there is no need for a hard sell.

A few tips to help you enhance your skills to cultivate trust in your relationships.
   a) Respect other's time
   b) Consider individual work styles
   c) Keep commitments
   d) Listen to their pain points and be solution focused
   e) Communicate clearly and openly
   f) Be transparent, if it doesn't work tell them
   g) Under promise and over deliver (or deliver the unexpected)

5. Let the doubt of others in your ability to succeed, motivate you.

Elle's boyfriend Warner broke up with her because she was too "blonde," however she was not going to let this or anything else stop her from getting admitted to Harvard Law. When she arrived at Harvard, she was judged based on her appearance. Being turned away from the smart crowd didn't faze her one bit. She created her own path for success.

In business and life, there will be judgers and haters. Let this be your motivator. No matter what you do, there will be people that support you and others that doubt your ability to succeed. You can choose to listen to those skeptics or just hit the "mute" button.

Marie sexton, a well-known fiction author, has a famous quote that goes like this; "You can't control what others think. The only thing you can control is yourself. Some people will look down on you for your choices in life, no matter what they are. You can't do anything about that. The only thing you can do is decide how to live your own life, and to hell with everybody else."

Here are a few ideas to keep doubters' thoughts from becoming your own self-limiting beliefs.

a) Use affirmations to align and remain positive.

b) Keep a positive attitude. Negativity spreads fast, so keep it under wraps.

c) Hear what the doubters say, listen to it, understand where it may be coming from then dismiss it. It might not be you they are doubting but it may be coming from a place of jealously, or other complications that you do not need to get yourself entwined in.

d) Use your failures as a propulsion to get it right the next time. We all learn from what we do. Just figure it out and do it better.

e) Avoid those Nay Sayers that are constantly at your door. Surround yourself with people who understand and support what you are doing on a more regular basis.

6. Finding a mentor who supports you is vital.

Professor Stromwell wanted nothing more than to see Elle succeed. When Elle was turned down by Warner and had a moment of weakness, Professor Stromwell told Elle, "If you're going to let one stupid prick ruin your life... you're not the girl I thought you were." We all need these individuals who are going to push us to be better and stronger.

Mentors are people who can and want to help you in your business and life. They will help you build leadership, value, and character. They can be from your own industry or not, they can be the same gender or not, it all depends on what you want to get out of the relationship. Mentoring is about the transfer of wisdom from one to another. The only requirement is that you pick someone that you can learn from. Someone that either has business knowledge you want to learn, or has done something you want to emulate.

According to Nicole Fallon, strong mentorship can provide an advantage for any professional at any career level, but for female professionals, especially those in leadership positions, a mentor can make all the difference. With the guidance of a trusted mentor, women can learn to overcome the internal and external factors that hold them back, and go on to successfully grow in their careers (Nola Hennessy, founder and CEO of Serenidad Consulting)

Criteria to consider when selecting a Mentor
1) Identify someone you admire and respect
2) A good active-listener
3) Truth-teller
4) Someone, who has different strengths than you
5) Know your mentoring needs, find someone who can add value
6) Someone with actual time with you

Remember you can have more than one mentor.

7. Take your time, learn the dynamics of your industry, don't give up, and learn to be productive.

Elle showed up to class on the first day with nothing but a pink notebook and fuzzy pen. She had not read the assignments and failed to answer questions when called on. Although she was embarrassed in front of her entire class and kicked out, this was not going to stop someone like Elle Woods. Instead, she got the supplies she needed, read the assignments, and impressed everyone with well-articulated answers in the next class.

We want to spend a bit of time on this topic. As we start to learn more about our new way of doing business, or even in the old way, we still have to look at our productivity and how we can accomplish more and do it faster and more productive.

Although neither Wendy nor Jessica are lovers of equations, they often have utilized the Pareto principle (80/20 rule) to help them identify priorities and have applied it to their businesses and life.

The Pareto Principle was named after the economist Vilfredo Pareto who found that 80% of the land in Italy was owned by just 20% of the population. In the 1940's Pareto's theory was advanced by Dr. Joseph Juran, an American electrical engineer who was widely credited with being the father of quality control. It was Dr. Juran who coined it "The Pareto Principle".

Currently when we talk about the 80/20 rule we are referencing the relationship between input and output. This means that roughly 80% of the effects of what you are doing come from 20% of the causes. Or in other words, 20% of the invested input is responsible for 80% of the results obtained.

Another application of the Pareto principle, constructed by Randy Mayeux, a corporate trainer, is the 96-minute rule, which maintains that knowledge workers should devote themselves to their most important tasks for that time period each day to improve their productivity. This was derived from taking 20% of time from an 8-hour work day (who does that anymore).

In utilizing this rule, workers should avoid multitasking and protect themselves from interruptions and distractions such as phone calls, email or anything else distracting. The first 96 minutes of the work day is considered the more effective, although it does vary from one individual to another.

This rule can significantly help you prioritize things within your business or your life. If you can figure out what 20% of your time produces 80% of your business results so you can spend more time on those activities and less time on others, leaving the rest of your time to do all the other things you want/like to do.

Now this doesn't mean you can just slack off and not do anything else that might create more business, but you want to spend the majority of your time on what makes the most sense to be successful.

We as business leaders often get pulled into many directions, whether it is a new program or venture or helping grow and teach others, we often have to stick with our plan to make sure we are continuing to meet our goals.

Wendy recalls many times when in the corporate environment, she had been pulled into strategy meeting after strategy meeting, and pulled to do multiple things for one of the growing programs she was dealing with, being called by numerous physicians that needed her immediate attention at the same time as she had to travel to other campuses to put together new programs.

It was almost as though she was standing in place, nothing appeared to be getting done as she didn't even know where to start. Her normal way of identifying things to get done was to write lists. The list had gotten to be around 50 items that she had to accomplish with probably more that she had forgotten. Knowing that she had to do a lot of those things and really could not completely delegate them or ignore them, she applied this rule and picked out the top 10 things and worked out a plan to accomplish them. Placing less emphasis on the others but continuing to have a plan to complete them either through delegation or holding off till some of the other things were off her plate then placing them higher up on that list. This not only helped Wendy feel better and more accomplished but allowed her to complete things more rapidly.

We find sometimes that things that end up on our list are just fillers, things that if given the time. Will fall off naturally. If we find ourselves working on things that are not meaningful and spending valuable time when we could be working on something that will be more impactful we feel like we have failed.

The 80/20 rule can apply to your life as well. If you review what you do on a daily basis we bet you will see how this is impacting your life. You spend a higher percentage of your phone calls with a small percentage of your contacts, you spend the biggest chunk of your money on a few things such as mortgage, car payment and you spend your time with a small percentage of people you know and so on. Why can't we all apply this to our core competencies and passions and make our work just as organized?

Jessica has described using this method to be able to handle all of her tasks at hand. She has successfully been able to segment her time and energy around what is more important in her business and life and what gets her the biggest return for that time. Jessica has really enjoyed writing and creating new opportunities for her business. She segments her time so that she can spend time on her new ventures, her work that she currently completes, and her family and friends. This has allowed her to DO IT ALL!

Although Wendy has had to do this in her work environment, she is still learning how to manage all of it together with the incorporation of the 80/20 rule into her personal and joint venture activities.

In a business sense, finding the 80/20 ratios is vital for maximizing performance. You will need to find the products or services that generate the most income/success and drop the rest that only provide marginal results. This way you can pick up more of what is benefiting you in your endeavors and get rid of those that are not supporting you. We can use this principle to continue to work on the core skills and leave the other tasks to others that are not as vital to your work. Work hardest on those things that are working hardest for you and your goals and achievements.

In utilizing these principles, you can start to breakdown and analyze your life and your work to see how best to have it all, and be successful at it. Be sure to ask yourself each time you begin focusing on something whether or not it will be in your top 20%.

8. "First impressions are not always correct."

You know that old saying, "never judge a book by its cover" well there is a great truth in it. At the core of every person that is substance. But you have to be willing to invest in the relationship, in order find it. In the movie, Elle's worst enemy, Vivienne Kensington, eventually became one of her best friends at Harvard. Why because Vivienne and Elle found commonality even though they were different.

What gets tricky is that most people believe that you have "30" seconds to make an impression on another person. In fact, new research is actually saying that it is more like "4" seconds to make the impression and then a total of "30" seconds for it to become ingrained in the other person as an opinion.

Although this may be truth in scientific study, life in community shows us a slightly different reality, particularly among us women. In most cases, we do get an additional chance to make an impression.

There are those times though, when others already formulate a preconceived belief about us from their own perspective. Wendy recalls one such example. Wendy was part of the C-Suite in one of the hospitals she worked. There was a monthly Stewardship meeting with the team where the Sr. VP of the area came to learn about the activities and performance of the campus. The Team prepared each month for this meeting, making sure that the agenda was perfect, that there was a cadence as to what was said and how it was said as to make sure the best side of the campus was portrayed as much as possible. It was pretty much an understanding that if you were not on the agenda you were not to discuss anything (or so Wendy thought). Since this was Wendy's first experience at this level she made sure to follow the directions as best she could. Wendy thought she was being successful as she was following what she understood to be the rules and only speaking up when she was on the agenda.

On one occasion, Wendy was asked for feedback on her boss, the CEO's performance for his annual review from the Sr. VP. Wendy met with her and after providing feedback on her boss she took the opportunity to ask the Sr. VP about her own performance and how she could do better. The Sr. VP proceeded to ask her if she liked her job and felt she was contributing as best she could. Wendy of course answered "yes" and asked why she would ask that. The Sr. VP then proceeded to tell her that she had not really seen her contributing in the meetings unless she was on the agenda and she felt that she might not be engaged in all of the activities of the campus. Astonished, Wendy indicated that was not the case at all and told her that since she was new she wanted to make sure she was learning all she could and may have not felt as comfortable speaking out (thinking that maybe she misinterpreted the rule). After the Sr. VP left Wendy vowed to make sure that her opinion was always heard and that she was observed as being interested and connected in all she did

Neuroscience research completed at New York University, led by Daniela Schiller reveals that impressions are formulated in the posterior cingular cortex and that the amygdala computes the sensory information that leads to the formulation of first impression. Meaning that information is sorted based upon its personal and subjective importance to you. Therefore, if you want to make a good impression on a person, give them a reason to like, trust and to value you.

So then how do we fix a bad first impression? Depending upon the value of the relationship to you, you ASK for feedback and based upon it, take action to correct the misperceptions and build upon that. All relationships take work, but not all relationships are workable or desirable.

9. Fight for what you believe in. Just learn about timing.

Women, use your intuition, guided by your values and principles, as well as beliefs. Some of these are innate and other learned. But the trick is to anticipate timing.

In the movie, Elle won her court case defending Brooke Wyndham, not because she followed the best defense, but because she followed her gut, which told her that Brooke was innocent and that there was more to her story. Even when all evidence pointed to Brooke's guilt, Elle stuck her ground.

Now in this example things turned out well, but in real life there are other factors to consider, which can ruin a career, cause a relationship or a business to fail—Timing.

Timing is critical. Do you stand your ground even at the risk of losing? Perhaps, but it depends upon what is at stake of being lost and whether or not that loss makes sense in that particular moment.

What should not be a factor is Fear, but all too often we do not put our hand up to speak, because we fear confrontation.

Key - make sure the battle is worth the fight and know the potential outcomes and be okay with all of them. Or find a more opportunistic time to voice your opinion when the stakes are not as high. Keep these points in mind and you will be able to navigate interactions with others well.

Being right is not always as important as being present, and perhaps right at another time.

10. Failure is an important part of the plan.

I'm sure you have heard this before, but we learn more from failure than success. The movie character, Elle certainly demonstrated that to us in a big way. She failed well and in no less than at Harvard.

The most important takeaway from failure, is that when done right, it is the building block for resilience. There will undoubtedly be several failures endured during life. These can either defeat you or strengthen you, so let's choose the latter.

Here are some handy ways to think opportunistically when reflecting on failure:

a) Self-talk is very impactful, filter out the negativity and find the silver lining and reaffirm it to yourself through positive self-talk
b) Mistakes are great for learning what not to do next time - refinement
c) Marginalize mistakes. Don't marginalize yourself because of mistakes
d) Make a mistake rather than do nothing at all
e) Use failure to fuel your next breakthrough
f) Take the mistake and leverage it to gain mentoring
g) When you fall, get up and do it better the next time

11. Leverage your "soft and fluffy" skills.

In legally blonde, Elle thrives on creating a vibrant environment wherever she goes. As head of the Delta Nu Sorority, Elle lives with her sorority sisters and head's many events, organizations, and social gatherings. She seeks connections with those around her and doesn't leap to judgement. The movie displays how Elle uses the abilities she has naturally in order to be successful. She reads people well and knows how to make people open up.

Not only is Elle open to new experiences, she also brings her personal street smarts to the court room. She doesn't drop her old way of thinking just to appear professional. Instead, Elle adapts her wit to the situation even when people scoff at her and think she's not thinking. She has a great talent for forging friendships and proves her loyalty and adamant attitude.

We can all take Elle's advice and use a little of our soft and fluffy skills to get ahead in our business and life. In many ways, our soft and fluffy skills are part of the uniqueness of our USP, and they encompass our attitudes, habits and how we interact with other people. They are much less tangible than hard or technical skills and unlike hard skills they are harder to learn. But not impossible!

CHAPTER 8: Ask and Serve to Find the Hidden Figures in Selling & Technology

UGH!! Numbers, Tech and Sales oh my!!

In the blockbuster feature Hidden Figures, we are introduced for the first time, to three remarkable Black American women, who were never recognized for their contributions to the NASA Space Program until 2015. Set in the early 1960's, these three marginalized Black American women mathematicians were working at the West Area Computing division, segregated from the rest of Langley Research Center, along with many other Black American women who worked as human computers (meaning they did math by hand). The NASA Space Program was in its infancy, still competing with their Russian counterpart, in trying to be the first in space. America did not win that competition, but were it not for the extraordinary analytical geometry skills of Katherine Goble 1969's Apollo 11 Flight to the moon and Apollo 13 would have never happened.

Mrs. Goble was awarded the Presidential Medal of Freedom in 2015, her first significant recognition for her tremendous contribution to American history. Her colleagues and close friends did not get left far behind. Dorothy Vaughan, a tenacious born leader taught herself IBM computation and analytics, then taught her colleagues so that their skills would not become obsolete, and became the first Black American Woman Supervisor of NASA Space Program Analysis & Computation Division. Mary Jackson broke barriers in education and pursued her engineering degree, a profession, at the time, reserved for White Men only. This movie was not only inspiring, but a reminder that not too long ago, women, a minority, were marginalized. We are only now starting to emerge and to be recognized for the extraordinary contributions we can make.

At no point in this movie, was the message of "Us versus them" depicted. Rather, the resonating message was we are stronger and better together, than apart and alone. This was a classic example of how we can leverage each other's strengths to collectively benefit.

The movie also provided a beautiful message to all women that we have to support and uplift each other, in order to promote and mentor those following in our footsteps.

How ironic that these women succeeded in mathematics and technology. Science Technology Engineering Mathematics (STEM) competencies are traditionally pursued disproportionately more by men than women. There has been speculation and research that has posited that this is due to the proliferation of the belief that women are not numerically or scientifically inclined. A more truthful statement might be that until recently girls/women were not typically encouraged to pursue studies in these subjects. This trend is slowly changing.

Let's figure out why Tech.

When was the first personal computer invented?

Answer; personal computer history doesn't begin with IBM or Microsoft, although Microsoft was an early participant in the fledgling PC industry. The first personal computers, was introduced in **1975**, it came as kits: The MITS**Altair 8800**, followed by the IMSAI 8080, an Altair clone. (Yes, cloning has been around that long).

When did the information highway get built?
Actually, what is it really?

Answer; in general, an internet is any network using TCP/IP (Transmission Control Protocol/Internet Protocol is the basic communication language or protocol of the Internet. It can also be used as a communications protocol in a private network [either an intranet or an extranet]). It was launched around the time when ARPANET was interlinked with NSFNET in the late **1980s**, and the term was used as the name of the network, Internet, being the large and global TCP/IP network.

Okay now that we have answered the 'What' and 'How'. Is it crystal clear?

Answer: as mud!

Ladies for our purposes, like with all other accessories in life, what we need to know, that is unless you are a tech geek, which if you are, can we get your number (just kidding), is:

1. What does it do for us?

2. How can we use it to leverage it to make our lives easier, more efficient, and productive?

However according to online bloggers [since Sex in the City blogging became the fastest growing media skill in the world], women entrepreneurs and aspiring women entrepreneurs say that their biggest challenges (pain points) with technology are:

(a) The lack of knowing and training around tech products.

(b) The never-ending changes and updates – hard to keep up.

The good news is that as more women become consumers and more female Tech Goddesses enter the marketplace, tech is becoming more user friendly. There is no longer a need to learn programming code, in order to build your website, create networks and to communicate on social media etc.

But let's not kid ourselves because for the newbie, even these ready-made platforms can be cumbersome and illogical. They just cannot do what our minds want them to. Can you guess why? Yup, it's because most app developers out there do not think with the feminine brain in mind.

However, there are basics that every entrepreneur must know about tech; because if you want your business to survive, a presence on the internet and a finite strategic marketing niche campaign is paramount.

When we looked at technology and what is needed for a start-up business, we grouped things into a few initial categories. The basics really.

7 – Start-up Technology Must Haves:

1. Hardware:

Please do the research. The following are suggestions, we are not affiliates of any of the products we list, and tech evolves quickly therefore do your homework peruse reviews and gauge your needs based upon your budget and lifestyle. But these are the basics.

a. Computer/laptop
b. Smart phone
c. External hard drive
d. Network Server (if you do not have cloud)
e. Wireless Router

f. Wireless Printer

2. Operating System:

The operating system (OS) allows users to perform the basic functions of a computer. The OS manages all software and peripheral hardware, and accesses the central processing unit (CPU) for memory or storage purposes. It also makes it possible for a system to simultaneously run applications. All PCs, laptops, tablets, smartphones, and servers require an OS. Developers may use specific operating systems that are more conducive to programming and application development, while the average employee will likely use a proprietary system for more common, everyday usage. The most common operating systems are Microsoft's Windows, Apple's OS X, Linux distributions, and mobile operating systems for smartphones.

3. Cloud Storage:

Cloud storage is a simple and scalable way to store, access and share data over the internet. It is maintained, operated, and managed by a cloud storage service provider on a storage server that is built on virtual techniques. Having cloud storage is simple and effective and the choice for most when saving files. However, we usually recommend having hard copy back up on things that you want to make sure you have forever.

Why you ask...because does anyone really know where the cloud is?

We can look up and see clouds, but we know that is not where our data is, or is it?

a. Dropbox
b. Google Drive

    c. Apple icloud

    d. Microsoft One Drive

    e. Box

4. Software: Organization and Productivity apps:

We all feel the need to be everywhere and do everything but still need something to keep us on track. It's not easy to stay on top of all your to-do, errands, and files and so on, fortunately for us, there are many tools available. Organizational and productivity apps are a must have. Whether it is just a calendar and task list or a full-blown project management tool, it is an essential tool. Here are a few examples (remember we are not affiliated with any of these products).

    a. Google Drive: lets you store and access your files anywhere

    b. Google Calendar: keep your appointments on track

    c. Evernote: a suite of software and services that allow users to capture, organize and

    find info across multiple platforms.

    d. Basecamp: project management tool that offers a variety of customer service options.

    e. Simple mind: a digital mind map that provides a space for all your ideas.

5. Customer Relations Management (CRM) AUTOMATION Applications

CRM's as they are called in tech marketing language, are vital to any business, and it is a critical application for women-owned small businesses that are customarily owner-all-operated at least at first. Today there are many that are specific to certain industries and there are those developed specifically with the small business in mind. CRM is a term that refers to practices, strategies and technologies that companies use to manage and analyze customer interactions and data throughout the customer lifecycle, with the goal of improving business relationships with customers, assisting in customer retention and driving sales growth. Here are a few examples

a. Infusionsoft

b. Ontraport

c. Salesforce

d. ACT

e. Nimble

f. Zoho

6. Principle Asset – Email List - AUTOMATION Application(s)

If your business is not ready for a full CRM, then email automation is the most effective way to engage in email marketing because it enables you to send out message broadcasts to your customers simultaneously and the best part, you can schedule them, so they go out even when you are not there.

Using automation, saves you time, and segmenting of your lists, based upon the responses of your recipient, allows you to continue very individualized and specific conversations with them. Result, you as the business owner can develop a closer relationship with your prospective or active customers by maintaining effective communication and brand awareness. Tech platform examples:

a. iContact

b. Constant Contact

c. Mailchimp: makes ending out a newsletter easy

d. Campainer

e. Aweber

f. Convertkit

7. Social Media & content tools/lead generators

Social media networks are a major resource for both small and big businesses that are looking to promote their brands on the Internet. The platforms are easy to use and some of them even have paid advertising options for businesses that want to reach new audiences. However, just because your business needs to be on these platforms doesn't mean that it has to be on every other social media site. To properly utilize the power of social media you need to know the most popular social media sites and identify the ones that work best for your business to avoid spreading yourself too thin.

Facebook the mammoth social media platform that revolutionized social networking and community building, where a member does not pay a penny. The win for Facebook is it has become the largest social networking site in the world with over 1.5 billion users worldwide. And today, Facebook has broken new ground in sales/marketing/advertising, as now savvy entrepreneurs can leverage the reach of Facebook through still relatively cost-effective advertising ads.

Google and Twitter although different types of social media are not doing too shabby themselves. However, unlike the 20th century users, who primarily posted pics of themselves, friends, pets and family, today well positioned advertisements are generating millions of dollars in return on investment for online (we like high-tech) entrepreneurs.

In March 2016, Facebook launched Facebook Live, the platforms integrated tool to connect people to people in a more real-time authentic manner. If you are camera shy, then you can also upload video on Facebook. The point, Cisco predicted that by 2019, about 80% of all consumer internet traffic will be generated by internet video traffic. That's staggering!

a. Facebook

b. Twitter

c. LinkedIn (professional networking)

d. Google+

e. YouTube

f. Pinterest (more than ½ of 100 million users are women)

Now that you have the basics covered, at least in terms of start-up tech tools and few basic connection point apps. We have to move the discussion to technology must-haves for your specific USP.

In prior chapters were discuss how to get to what is your USP and to what are you selling? Check and check.

If, you are still not sure where to find a niche. Here are a few leads. According to Inc., in an article published that interviewed experts and examined investment data, the top industries were identified that are beginning to offer major opportunities for new ventures. Here are the ones that hold the most promise in 2017:

1. **Meditation and mindfulness training**: increased corporate spending on programs to improve employee focus has helped boost an industry that research firm IBISWorld values at $1.1 billion in the U.S. App-based training is bringing the practice to an even broader audience.

2. **Ready-to-Drink coffee and tea**: Consumers are ditching mixes and concentrates in favor of on-the-go coffee and tea, largely driven by health innovations. From 2013 to 2015, U.S. sales of these drinks

nearly tripled, landing at $143 million, according to the nonprofit Specialty Food Association.

3. **Mobility Tech**: The industry offers startups potential partnerships with and acquisition by large tech companies and automakers working on autonomous vehicles. Ford for example, invested $1 billion in Pittsburgh-based Argo AL in its effort to develop a self-driving car by 2021.

4. **Pet Care**: Tech innovations are making over this industry, which is valued at $60 billion in the U.S. Revenue for pet grooming and boarding alone was nearly $8 billion in the U.S. in 2016, according to IBISWorld, which projects it to grow 7 percent annually through 2021.

5. **Construction Management**: Global funding for hardware and software to streamline building projects, or to sell and rent construction equipment, rose to $254 million in 2015 from $51 million in 2010, according to researcher CB insights and analysts say it's' still an emerging industry.

6. **Synthetic Biology**: Health and environmental concerns have driven interest in genetically engineered medicines, foods, and fuel. It's a costly and technical field, but payoffs can be huge.

7. **Computer Vision**: Advancements in artificial intelligence have produced companies working to interpret and act on visual data. The technology, which attracted $522 million and 69 deals in 2016 can be applied to child development, social media networks, and web analytics.

8. **Brick-and-mortar Retail** Technology: Startups are helping modernize in-store operations to compete with ecommerce.

Now that we've shared the top-8 industries with promise of opportunity go and explore, research, and create your niche, based upon your passion.

But, if you need further guidance, we are going to deliver even more, the fasting growing Passive income generating industries is, drum roll please: Whatever Industry you currently have some competence in – a combination of your refined soft and hard skills.

You might be wondering what we mean by that. Well simply creating Digital and Information-Based products is the most profitable way of making money on the internet. Thousands of bloggers, freelancers and skilled professionals make sustainable passive income by selling digital products on their blogs, or different digital marketplaces. Just check out this link if you think you have nothing to offer, we dare you:

https://realpassiveincomeideas.com/information-product-examples/

Individuals are making millions by sharing intellectual property, by over-delivering and adding value to others, who have an interest in improving themselves, their business, or their life. And so can you!

The next section of our conversation is going to assume that you, like us, want to make passive income for yourself and your families through your business.

What technology do you need, you ask?

The answer is, it depends. Remember your unique selling proposition, you will provide your "what", and then your target of "who "you will serve, determines the technology you need. Yes, that and of course your budget.

But, in essence there are a couple of sure-and-tried roadmap tracks to getting into the online business industry by developing Digital and Information-Based products.

First, the reason information is valuable is because there is an audience that needs your solution. Therefore, start with the end in mind – The Solution. But do not build a product, until you have tested the market. The way to do that is through a strategic lead magnet.

The magnetic power of the lead magnet

A lead magnet is an irresistible ethical bribe offering a specific chunk of value to a prospect in exchange for their contact information. The goal of the Lead Magnet is to maximize the number of targeted leads you are getting for an offer. More times than not if you can offer a value-added freebie that is a lead into your buyer's journey, the return on investment (because there is money involved) improves.

The lead magnet today, is like the use of focus-group product testing in the olden days LOL. An advertisement campaign.

However, today this is a low-cost investment to determine whether your solution to a problem (pain-point) gains traction in the market. This is a reverse engineered strategy, because in traditional advertising, you create a campaign around your products, to market them, and you promote your brand recognition. If the campaign is successful then your number of units sold will skyrocket, due to successful brand recognition and identification.

Today, advertisement on the internet using a lead magnet has to be viewed as an investment, not a cost, because what you are actually purchasing is a prospective customer that you will need to nurture for a period of time, providing them with value content on a regular basis, most would suggest daily, in order to establish likability, value, and trust.

This strategy typically has an initial low conversion rate (meaning leads converting into customers), but over time, through community building, the return on investment (ROI) improves. The reason for this is that unless you have brand recognition [Apple, FB, Tony Robbins...], you are starting the conversation with a new acquaintance.

Remember the conversation we had on the 80/20 rules? This comes totally into play in the nurturing of your acquaintances (leads). A superb efficient lead magnet attracts serious potential buyers of your product; and differentiates those people that are just browsing and have no real intention to engage. (5)

According to research, 50% of the leads in any system are not ready yet to buy. Almost 80% of new leads never become sales, but the good news, nurtured leads make 47% larger purchases than non-nurtured leads (5). Therefore nurturing the right, warm, leads is a best practice for your sales/marketing campaign.

Now that is not to say that with a very refined USP, a niche (not yet over saturated) that is well sought after, your ROI would perform better than average. That is why your unique selling proposition the solution to the pain point has to be very well defined.

Another way to think of strategic lead magnets is, as door openers.

Low vs High Ticket Information-Based Products

When Information-Based products broke into the internet marketplace they were typically ebooks and membership site with member's only content libraries. Companies such as Clickbank,

Gumroad, Leanpub, eJunkie and Amazon (kindle space) and other similar eCommerce product affiliate marketing platforms were created.

Products sell on these platforms for as little as 0.99 cents/per unit. However, with increasing emergence and sophistication of LMS (Learning Management Software) information-based product producers began establishing their own universities and academies online. These platforms are licensed therefore they also have access to data pools to extrapolate what is working and what is not in terms of sales and ROI data.

The most recent findings from the larger players in the LMS space has been that High-Ticket products have a better conversion rate, because it simply takes fewer sales to earn more. However, the delivery of these higher priced items require mastery of the over 24 psychological triggers of selling. The vehicle most commonly used by high-ticket markers is the virtual sales letter (VSL) through a live or recorded webinar.

A webinar currently is the highest converting marketing strategy in the internet marketplace today. A well scripted VSL presented live, with face-to-face contact, multiple times during high-traffic time zones and dates can earn you thousands of dollars in a few minutes, as compared to having to nurture a relationship over time. The key, Over Deliver on a highly sought after solution or teach a hard skill for the vocation of internet marketing.

Over the last year, Jessica has sat in on hundreds of top-notch VSL webinar offerings and has witnessed how marketers earn themselves or their clients' $50-100,000.00 over a series of 4-6 repeat webinars (in a week).

Top Reviewed Webinar Software

a) Onstream Webinars
b) Cisco WebEx
c) Weinato
d) Adobe Connect
e) Click Webinar

So now that you sold your first information-based product, and you have a customer, know that once a customer has bought from you once, they are 75% more likely to buy from you again. So, what do you think you should be doing? Like with any relationship continue the conversation. Ladies we like to talk therefore this is not difficult for us.

Remember just earlier in this chapter we provided a few automation tools to help you maintain an active conversation with your new prospective customers. Okay leverage the technology to deliver content rich email/blogs conversation to them on a regular basis.

In the movie Dorothy, no not the Wizard of Oz character, the one in Hidden Figures, Dorothy had to update her mathematical skills and she had to transfer that knowledge to computer assisted computation. Similarly, if you want to survive in entrepreneurship leveraging the internet, you will need to transfer your "soft fluffy skills" into a new media. That is of course if you pursue a passive income through production of information-based products.

There are other products, such as a new invention, the no-mess, clips or comb hair extensions. Jessica saw an advertisement launched by Daisy Fuentes selling just that. Think home-shopping network channels and now transfer those goods to the internet through an e-store platform.

Another option out there, Jessica and Wendy both have observed how individuals, who are not interested in creating anything are still making money on the internet, by selling other people's products. These types of relationships are called affiliates. No this is not the same as multilevel marketing schemes of the 1980's and beyond. Although we cannot lie, it does have somewhat of an air of familiarity to it.

Affiliate marketing is a new terminology for an online salesperson. Some companies offer a one-stop shop, where they provide you a link to promote and sell. Then you as their salesperson receive a commission on every referral or unit that you sell for them. However, you have to either market it to your company asset (email list) or use paid advertisement to get leads in the door. You could make a living as an affiliate of many products, if you enjoy marketing and sales through the web.

There are also joint-venture opportunities on the web, for those individuals, who have a product, but no customer base, and prefer to partner with an online marketer, who has an extensive email list (50,000+) or other leverage point. The key to this strategy is cross marketing of another person's product that you trust and know. The commission split on these types of deals can run typically about 50/50.

However, in this later scenario as the newbie product owner, the venture is win/win because you push out your offering into the marketplace; and also gain access to a more robust email list of future customers in the process. The conversion rate on this type of sales strategy is much higher than 3-5%, which is typical ROI on independent product launches to a cold new prospect list of customers.

Speaking to Sell with Kid Gloves – No Hard Sells Here

Every business depends upon the ability to sell. However, there is an art to it, and as women we are gifted gabbers, but speaking to sell requires learning the art of storytelling. Insider secret ladies, the best way to convert cold traffic, into warm prospects is to use your gift to tell your story, in the most transparent manner possible.

Being able to resonate with others on an emotional level is the number one psychological trigger that turns a prospect into your loyal customer. And we do it naturally. Put two ladies in a room, give them a few snacks, drinks of any kind, and be the fly on the wall, and observe what happens. As the ladies begin to get to know each other, they find points of synergy and then off they go. They can talk for hours.

In business however, the gift of connecting with others on an emotional level has to be refined to a simplistic solution-focused message, delivered in the most succinct manner possible. Now that is a challenge for most of us. Because telling the story requires all the necessary (or presumed needed) details.

Our advice, and we don't give it often, because we prefer that others formulate their own opinions based upon the information provided, is "less is more." Research findings tell us that the average attention span of an adult today is no more than that of a goldfish (less than 8 seconds, Times Health 2014), therefore get to the solution first, then depending upon the quality of your engagement, provide as much detail as permitted. Use interactive tools, as people learn differently. If possible integrate visual, auditory, and tactile stimulation, but if all you have is a live stream video, then learn the power of active listening, body language, eye contact; and of words to engage others.

As women remember we are created with nature ability to develop those vital connections to others, by using intuitive and emotional intelligence, we can nurture and develop community. Social platforms provide virtual meeting places where you don't have to leave the comfort of your home in order to connect with like-minded-hearted individuals. Private Facebook pages and private member sites are just a few of the places you can not only build but privately communicate with your tribe.

Another skill that is valuable in speaking to sell is to actively listen to your community members' conversations; and identify their repeated questions, or the woes that are commonly shared. This vital information can then be used to formulate a solution. It is really important to get the next point, do not speak in great deal about how to get to the solution, initially. The truth is that the people with the pain point first just want to know there is a solution; and that you have it for them. Simplicity is key. Jessica once heard the analogy made that people don't want to know all the science behind how to use a hammer to make a hole in the wall, just that the hole, anchors your beautiful picture, just right.

There will be time for the details, during a well prepared Virtual Sales Letter or persuasive sales story. In fact, Dan Kennedy, one of the best-known platform salesmen was quoted as saying, "Sometimes a marketable speech only needs to be storytelling" to be persuasive, but timing is everything. We would add that authenticity and credibility, due to authority is also paramount. Kennedy likes to go for the shock approach, to engage, like several other platform speakers in the space. That is not our approach.

As we discussed in a prior chapter, today authority and credibility have less to do with one's hard skills and credentials and more to do with efficiency, simplicity and being solution-focused. And of course, making offerings easily accessible, user friendly and that over deliver. However, you will not even be able to solve the pain point/problem for your customer, if you cannot close the sale. The key is that your lasting impression is from the way you start and the way you end your sales story (Kennedy, 2016).

In her book "Women make the Best Salesmen", Maron Luna Brem, went from finding out she had cancer with no health insurance nor husband, to owning multiple car dealerships with million dollar sales solely on her figuring out the secret of sales. She indicated that we are always selling whether it is for a job interview, getting our children into a good school, or operating a register at a department store or looking for a lifelong companion. She stipulates that women with their natural social skills and acute emotional antennae have a natural advantage that everyone can learn from.

The 7 Feminine Ingredients needed in a Sales Story to boost Sales

1. **Do not be afraid to self-promote**- no matter what the product, you are actually selling "You". You are setting the example of truth and trust and you must let the customer know that you would do whatever you can to make sure they get the right product. You're building credibility.

2. **Be authentic and transparent**- promote confidence in what you are selling and that you are honest. If the product is not for them, say it.

3. **Do not under value yourself or your service**- Remember money is an exchange for value added. The more No's you get the closer you are from "Yes," so embrace the No's and forge forward that was not the customer for you.

4. **Ask for help if you need it**- We have a tendency to not want to ask for help, thinking it will somehow make us weak and seem unprofessional. This is just not true. None of us know everything, that's why we have partners, mentors and friends. If we need it, ask for it. It will only help us with our personal growth.

5. **Keep the sale the priority**- often we have a tendency to spend too much time on relationships with the sales prospect. When the client rejects the sale, instead of educating them on why they

really need it (keeping the pitch going) go back to forging the relationship.

6. **Do not be afraid of making a mistake**-we are all "eternal perfectionists". We do not want to let anyone down, not even people we don't know personally. Above all we do not want anyone thinking we don't know what we are doing. That being said, we often play it safe. We hedge around the essential point of the sale, or use the pitch that worked before but not really hitting the pain point of our customers because it might not be right or it might be uncomfortable for them, thus potentially losing the deal. We must take the chance and use those big wild ideas we have and know by getting that YES, you are solving the person's pain point.

7. **Detach from the outcome**-Remember it's not you they are saying "No" to, it's the product or the process. Use phrases that just assume they are moving forward with the sale. "Now, how would you like to get started?" Guide them to the "Yes".

Build on your strengths and delegate the rest. Customers want to believe in the efficacy of the product and the person they are purchasing it from, therefore find the right vehicle to communicate that effectively. If you are camera shy, then videotape, blog, record audio. If the camera loves you, even if you don't love it, learn to script, rehearse and to deliver your unique message. There are thousands if not millions of people, especially women waiting to hear it. That is why, the USP, has to be a calling, bigger than just about you and a sale. Because it's that passion that will resonate far more, even at times, than the words; and it is passion that will fuel your success even through stage fright.

If we look at some of the ventures Wendy and Jessica have collaborated on, and bring you behind the veil, you'll learn that often times, Jessica has been selling without intent from the first words out of her mouth, and when the customer has bought into their added-value service based approach, Jessica has often turned to Wendy and said, "We can deliver that right?" They have a track record of over-delivering (Dr. Carter, Banner Hospital, Dr. Varnedore, Florida Hospital, Dr. Fernandez, Dean, Barry University, Irene Yanis, Citrus Hospital System). How do we do it? In the moment, there is an implicit trust between us that overrides any fear of selling.

Take our most recent trip down to the Peruvian Amazon. Although not necessarily a business venture (on the surface), Jessica informed Wendy of her intentions to take a self-discovery trip into the heritage of the Shipibo Tribal people to further deepen her exploration of the ancient healings of plant medicines, as well as to further conversation for collaborative mission work. Although extremely leery, Wendy agreed to do something that was very outside her comfort zone, because she trusted Jessica and felt that no matter whatever fears she might have personally, together they would be able to overcome anything. After the amazing trip, Wendy remarked that the experience was predicated on one of Jessica's best sales pitches ever...But also that it was one of Wendy's best buy-ins!

You might be asking yourself how you get started.

How do you use your communication skills pragmatically for sales?

The nuts and bolts, are basically that we are more wired to cross connect and build relationships then to do hard sales. We are more geared towards being inclusive and relational. Therefore, leverage these strengths, by asking more questions. Try to get to know the person on a more intimate level and use "tag" endings that compel responsive communication; i.e. "I know that you are having this issue, how can I help?"

In contrast, men are more interruptive, use a louder voice with inflection around the points, use less emotion, and stay on topic more but do not get personal.

Having this ability to connect with your clients provides a huge advantage in getting to know them and depending upon what your product is, to keep them in the relational realm for a longer timeframe.

Precautions, if you are selling to a man be cognizant of the typical differences in our communication styles, men respond better to factual content. Also, maintain the sales' call focus, and do not get so distracted by the intimate nature of the call that it becomes a chat.

How to Combine Logical Thinking with Intuition

As discussed, women have a greater ability to tap into social situations and provide interpersonal judgment when interacting with others. This gives us an advantage when selling as we can adjust our sales story by actively listening to your prospects' dialogue. According to a Harvard Business School professor, Gerald Zaltman, 95 % of our purchase decisions take place unconsciously. This is to say that we often intuitively reach a conclusion based upon our emotional responses which then we back up with a logical reason.

Connect Emotions with Memories

Establish an emotional link, through empathy and through reciprocity of expressed emotion. Since your lead magnet targeted your ideal customer, you'll be able to connect on a deeper level. Women make up 80% of the consumers of goods and services therefore we resonate due to an experience of collective consciousness.

An example, when Wendy purchased her "big house" it had everything to do with the agent's ability to know Wendy's dream of retiring in the home, bringing in the grandchildren as they arrived, hosting lots of events for their friends and family and being comfortable and safe. Hint the agent was a woman. Although all good real estate agents know that if married, the women of the house need to love the kitchen, bathrooms and closets, otherwise there is no chance of a sale.

Consequently, when providing a solution for a pain-point, you already know your prospective consumers' solution, therefore paint the picture and tap into the emotions utilized to create memories and close the sale. (4) After all you know that your customer will be better off because of it. And knowing that makes selling, not 'Salesie' at all.

Automating Sales

Like every other segment of the buyer's journey we have been outlining, sales can be automated through a relatively newly named internet process, Marketing Funnels. This tech terminology simple means automating the buyer's journey by brain mapping the sequences based upon buyer's response patterns.

Sounds easy right, it isn't. In fact, in an article published in September, 2016, the problem encountered with tradition one-lane fits all for all prospects is that we treat all prospects the same way, even though we know that they are on different tracks on their journey towards becoming customers.

According to Scott Oldford, of INFINITUS, either we take a broad approach, trying to appeal to anybody or everybody, hoping something will stick. Or we only reach out to "warm" markets who are already looking for the solution we provide and are one trigger away from making a purchase. The broad approach makes us spend way too much money and effort to get precious few buyers. And the warm approach makes us miss the opportunity to reach those who are early in their buying journey (2016).

That's why like with everything that is evolving, you have to think about marketing funnels differently. Oldford coined a strategy, typically used today (and we like the analogy and the logic of the approach), called the SSF Method and it entails creating different funnels for people who are on different lanes: the sidewalk, the slow lane, and the fast lane.

People on the Sidewalk fit the demographic of your target market. However, they are still largely unaware of the problem you can solve for them. They're experiencing the problem, alright, but they're not yet at the point where it's a nagging itch they want to scratch. They don't know about you (and don't care), and so they're far from being ready to purchase anything from you.

People on the Slow Lane are aware of the itch. They're starting to scratch, and they want to find a solution before it gets worse. But they want to make an informed choice. As such, they're actively seeking information and looking up to authority figures to show them the way.

Finally, **people on the Fast Lane** are acutely aware of the itch. In fact, it's keeping them awake at night, their skin is raw, and people are beginning to stare. So they're ready to purchase a solution, as long as it meets their needs and overcomes their objections.

Using this train of thought, Wendy and Jessica, and their collaborative team (including highly evolved men) have been working on a solution. And wouldn't you know it, it's been thought of, sort of: "Deliver an experience that will be so relevant, your lead won't be able to say 'NO,' Oldford advises. And the way to be relevant is to create a separate funnel for each of the three tracks. That means your job is different for each funnel: Don't ignore those who are on the Sidewalk. Get in their radar and show them what will happen if they don't take care of that itch soon.

For people on the Slow Lane, your job is to become the authority they're looking for. And for people on the Fast Lane, your task is to overcome their objections and show them how you're the best option they should get rid of that itch, once and for all. The funnels are also connected to each other: it should naturally lead people from the Sidewalk to the Slow Lane, and from the Slow Lane to the Fast Lane."

Make sense? Now to make the process automated you can use any of the CRM platforms we mentioned that have integrated marketing components. Or there are software applications/platforms specifically geared primarily to help you build marketing campaigns. Here are a few examples:

    a. ClickFunnels
    b. ProfitBuilder
    c. InfusionSoft
    d. Ontraport

Technology Needed to Close the Sale

1. Carts - Payment

As you create active or passive income, you have to have an integrated way to capture payments. Although we can still use cash and or checks, your business is not going to flourish unless you step up and get into the world of virtual payment methods. Paper and coins are going out of business. The new norm is online and easy. Although sometimes too easy, so we must make sure we have a secure site for our customers. You should look for a few types of online payments since not everyone may have the same type.

Here are a few examples:

a. PayPal

b. Square

c. Shopify

d. Amazon Payments

e. Direct bank or credit card processing

f. Bitcoin

2. Accounting – bookkeeping made easy

No matter what type of business you may have or want it is essential that you keep good track of your revenue and expenses in an organized fashion. Having a good software program will make both you and your accountant happy when it comes to filing your taxes, paying your bills, and earning your money and coming out squeaky clean if an audit were to ensue.

a. Here are a few examples:

b. Quick books

c. Quicken

d. Sage

e. NetSuite

Mary, Dorothy and Katherine, in the movie the Hidden Figures portrayed very strong-minded and willed young women, who knew their worth, even while everyone else marginalized them. They not only knew their worth, but they demonstrated it, through every opportunity afforded to them or ingeniously created by them. The uniqueness and applicability of the themes in the film lent themselves perfectly, to the emerging increase of women-owned technology science based small business. Not only are we seeing that more women are pursuing education and careers in technology and science, but they are venturing into high-tech entrepreneurship either by developing applications or by becoming savvy end-users to leverage their existing business scope. Take a look at this interesting link that show cases a few female-founded tech start-ups: Top female tech start-ups

Onward and upward ladies!

CHAPTER 9: Step Out to Step In

What would you do if you were not afraid?

The answer is nothing!

If we have accomplished our goals with this book, we hope that we dispelled the belief that fear is only experienced by you. Because that is just not truth. Fear is a collective experience, every single person on this planet has fears. What is most important to us is that we have inspired and empowered, as well as equipped you to have courage to walk through fear to your next breakthrough.

Stated a little differently by Wendy, "Don't be perceived as reckless, in your attempt to present fearless. Be cognizant of risk, but be brave and take action".

Socrates put it this way, "Courage (bravery) is knowing what not to fear, meaning that we should be afraid of some things but we can overcome those things that are not life-threatening and live our lives." And we would add…be less worried about what people think of us and get up and just do it!

The reality is that we cannot be without total fear, but it can be managed and even used to fuel us to pursue our dreams. Andrea Sachs & Miranda Priestly (Devil Wears Prada) depict strength of character, although different, but both committed to their passion-purpose and show us how to get the job done, without losing sight of who they are.

Kate Reddy and her husband (I Don't Know How She Does it?) exemplified what can be accomplished through a collaborative partnership when choices are made to live a dream life in balance.

Although there remain gender stereotypic perceptions we as a culture are slowing shifting the paradigm, by recognizing that gender specificity in terms of roles in a family system can be shared and at times reversed. We are evolving.

Margaret Tate (The Proposal) personifies the professional woman, who is afraid of intimacy, because she has been in the rat race for so long, but she too makes a choice and finds love in the process. And we added, takes the leap into entrepreneurship naturally. As most women do, Margaret has an abundance of transferable skills that can be utilized to fill a gap in the marketplace to serve others.

Liz Gilbert (Eat, Love, Pray), takes us all on a journey of self-discovery that spans the globe, how decadent, and real of all women, who strive to live life authentically and fully. We need to plan that next trip into the world. Stretch ourselves beyond what is expected and move into what is desired. And know that we deserve it.

Lena, Brash, Tibby and Carmen (The Sisterhood of the Traveling Pants) remind us of the importance and life enriching experience of community, our unique sisterhood. And how we are all interconnected and responsible for one another. They teach us quite simply that it is the diversity of our differences that we need to leverage to nurture and to benefit one another, instead of competing.

And of the feisty, trail blazing women breaking ground, Erin Brockovich, Elle Wood (Legally Blonde) and Katherine Goble, Dorothy Vaughan and Mary Jackson (Hidden Figures), these women inspire all of us to Step-Out to Step-In. We have to continue to build on women who have gone before us, fought for our rights, liberties and advancements in arenas not typically gender welcoming. Who are breaking down gender biases and setting a path for the next generation to improve upon.

FEARLESS does not mean the absence of fear but the ability to identify it, accept that it is present in our life, and move through it. STEP IN!! Step right into the middle of it and build on your God given strengths:

1. Communication – Language and expressive verbal skills
2. Power Combination – Logical Thinking and Intuition
3. Emotional Intelligence and Memory – Storytelling
4. Nurturers
5. Master Taskers

Wendy and Jessica shared their unique life journey experiences through family, love, work, and business, as they have a passion-purpose to build a tribe of likeminded-socially conscious women, who want to impact community in very tangible real ways. We believe that there is a special golden nugget in every single one of our sisters. We want to use our combined experience, knowledge and assets to inspire our sisters to Educate. Empower. Evolve.

By leveraging your intellectual property, creating a product, and taking a leap of calculated risk into online entrepreneurship, Wendy and Jessica believe that you will create passive or active income for your household and/or existing business. Financial market trends reveal that every person and business uses the internet for consumer-ship. More and more companies are forgoing brick-and-mortar positioning in favor of increased virtual ecommerce. The fastest growing industries all have a tech component.

Even our children today, seem to be born with a technology know-how from infancy. Jessica is no longer amazed when she observes two and three year olds playing on their parent's cellular telephone or their own tablet with proficiency. This is the world we live in, and it is only progressing towards artificial intelligence and automation of just about everything including driving a car.

Yet, we as women have pain points around tech and selling. Therefore, we provided tools and strategies that you can use to get started. But we know there is more needed and to provide a unique solution we have built a platform to make the process of Digital Information-Based Products and ecommerce YaYa-sister friendly.

Annually, we release the Dr. J. Millionaire-Made Entrepreneur Incubator Challenge. Application to the program, which involves successful completion of an intensive 12-week interactive, hands-on course, in soft and hard skills training in entrepreneurship, is the pre-requisite. Through this online course, you will not only learn all you need, in order to have a firm foundation in your small business, but you will receive guidance from some of the top leading professionals in business today in finding your niche, positioning your USP, developing your product and a strategic business and growth plan. From the entries (they are limited) the top 10 are picked and have an opportunity to pitch to a panel of independent capitalists, who are eager to fund new women-owned ventures. Join our private community at ElitePerformanceAcademy.us/EntraBiz-Club to be the first to be notified when the application process re-opens next.

There is additional motivation (not that empowering women is not a big enough motivator but), behind Wendy and Jessica's passion and as we are always transparent, everything that we are doing is not only about you and us, Wendy, Jessica and their partners, have chosen to take on the fight of their life, to eradicate an enemy that is enormous, as it is the fastest growing criminal industry and one of the greatest social pandemics in our generation – the exploitation and enslavement of women and children in the sex trade. Their game plan is to leverage the technology, the very portal vehicle that is currently used to sell our children online, and to utilize it to build an army of fiscally sound socially-conscious entrepreneur members.

Through their nonprofit, Elite Foundation – EliteFundsFreedom.org we are building a global platform that is dedicated to recover, rehabilitate and restore victims of this heinous crime.

Our goal is to fund the freedom of 1,000,000 souls by the year 2027. In today's economy, it costs approximately $150.00 to free one victim from the sex trade internationally. But, domestically the cost to rescue, rehabilitate and to restore a victim of Human Trafficking is exponentially more. Join us and donate generously 100% of all resources go to victim services: www.EliteFundsFreedom.org

Ladies it is a unique time in history, we are gaining recognition and positioning in all segments of finance, business, entrepreneurship, leadership, and in the family. We have momentum and it is each of our responsibility to mentor others, to become a voice for the voiceless, and to take on social injustice. Lock-shields with us and we will get this done!

Join Wendy, Dennis, and Jessica on their private Facebook page; https://www.facebook.com/EliteFundsFreedom/ for all the details on how you can get involved.

Resources for Women Entrepreneur

To support the growth of women starting and growing businesses, a robust ecosystem has been building itself out. Here are just some of the organizations that are available to you.

High-growth women entrepreneurs: Accelerators, boot camps and leadership training for women entrepreneurs include Dream it Athena, EY Entrepreneurial Winning, Merge Lane, Million Dollar Women Workshop, Springboard Enterprise and Women's Startup Lab (which just raised over $1 million in a Series A financing round). Networking organizations and organizations that connect women entrepreneurs to investors include Astia, Dell Women's Entrepreneur Network (DWEN), The Vinetta Project and Women 2.0. Mackenzie Burnett of Distributed Systems put together this list of angel and early-stage tech investors.

Small to mid-sized companies: Networking groups include Chic CEO, Ellevate, the National Association of Women Business Owners, Savor the Success, She Owns It, SheWorx, The Boss Network, and Womancon. Educational support includes Hello Fearless, Rent the Runway Project Enterprise, Tory Burch Fellows Competition, Women's Business Enterprise National Council (WBENC) and other organizations that certify women-owned businesses, Women Presidents' Organization (WPO), Women's Business Centers represent a national network of nearly 100 educational centers throughout the United States.

Federal small-business grants for women

The federal government offers some grants for small-business owners, but they're designated for very specific purposes, such as certain research and development projects or for businesses in rural areas. Government grants can't be used to cover startup costs or day-to-day expenses, and most aren't earmarked specifically for women.

1. Grants.gov

Grants.gov is a database of all federally sponsored grants. You can search for small-business grants here — just make sure you filter the results on the left side of the page to view grants specifically for small businesses.

2. InnovateHER Challenge

The U.S. Small Business Administration hosts an annual competition for businesses with a marketable product or service that positively affects women's lives. To participate, you must first enter and win a local InnovateHER Challenge to advance to the national semifinal round. The top three national finalists will win $40,000, $20,000 and $10,000, respectively.

3. Small Business Innovation Research and Small Business Technology Transfer programs

The SBA facilitates these two competitive programs, which ultimately provide grants to small businesses that contribute to federal research and development. Eleven federal agencies, including the departments of Agriculture, Defense, and Health and Human Services, post grant opportunities on their websites. You can search all grant opportunities on the SBIR website.

Insider tips: Sign up for our monthly small-business newsletter.

State and local small-business grants

Because federal small-business grants are limited in number and often very competitive, you may have better luck looking for grants at the state and municipal levels. You'll have to do your own research to pinpoint specific grant programs in your area, but here are some places to look:

4. Women's Business Centers

The SBA sponsors about 100 Women's Business Centers nationwide, designed to help women entrepreneurs with business development and access to capital. Some, such as the California Capital Financial Development Corp., lend money directly, while others simply help you find small-business grants and loans that you may qualify for.

5. Economic development agencies

Every state and many cities have economic development agencies focused on promoting a strong local economy. Even if the agency itself doesn't offer a small-business grant, it will likely be able to point you in the right direction.

6. Small Business Development Centers

There are hundreds of these SBA-sponsored centers around the country, typically housed at colleges and universities. SBDCs offer free, one-on-one business consulting. Set up a meeting with your local SBDC advisor, who will be able to tell you about grants and other business financing opportunities in your area.

Private small-business grants for women

Some private organizations and businesses have created national grant programs for women small-business owners. Here are two to look into:

7. Amber Grant

The Amber Grant Foundation awards $500 to a different women-owned business every month. At the end of each year, one of the 12 grant winners is awarded an additional $2,000. The application is relatively simple: Explain what your business is, describe what you'd do with the grant money and pay a $7 application fee. The foundation's advisory board chooses the winners, looking for women with passion and a good story.

8. Eileen Fisher Women-Owned Business Grant

Eileen Fisher, a women's clothing retailer, awards $100,000 to up to 10 women business owners each year. To be eligible, women must make up at least 51% of your business's ownership and leadership, your business must have been in operation for at least three years, it must not exceed $1 million in annual revenue, and it must be focused on environmental or social change.

Two other good possibilities for grants

These options aren't specifically for women, but they're good small-business grants to consider:

9. FedEx Small Business Grant

FedEx awards up to $25,000 apiece to 10 small businesses annually. The application requires an explanation of your business, how you'd use the money, photos of your business and — this part is optional — a short video explaining your business. You don't need a FedEx account to apply.

10. Mission Main Street Grants

Chase Bank gives $150,000 to 20 small businesses each year through its Mission Main Street Grants program. To be eligible, you must have been in business at least two years and have fewer than 100 employees, and the application includes answering five essay questions.

More: Find small-business grants for minorities

Angels and Venture Capitalist Opportunities

Female Funders aims to activate 1000 female accredited investors to make their first angel investment.

Plum Alley Investments offers male and female accredited investors a way to invest in outstanding companies led by women entrepreneurs and gender diverse teams.

Radical Generosity from SheEO started in Canada and will roll out to several cities throughout the U.S. in 2016. One thousand women in a city contribute $1,000 each to raise $1 million per fund, which will be provided as interest free loans to 10 women-led companies.

The Mel Rines '47 Student Angel Investment Fund teaches female undergraduates at the University of New Hampshire how to manage an investment fund.

The Rising Tide Fund uses a "learn-by-doing" model. Accredited female investors make small stake investments in companies raising money via Portfolia, a crowdfunding platform for consumer products.

Other training organizations include 37 Angels, Pipeline Angles (now in 21 cities) and Women First from Angel Resource Institute. The rise in the number of women angels is great for early stage women-led companies, but it is venture firms that will provide growth capital, said Amoils. As the hiring of Joanna Drake Earl demonstrates, angels are a source for VC partners.

ABOUT THE AUTHORS

Jessica Vera, is a Trauma-Survivor, Mother, and a Wife with a PhD, who lives in Florida and was born in Peru. For years she struggled with the feeling she wasn't good enough and didn't deserve to be happy. She was fear-filled. Then she discovered where these feelings came from and that she wasn't the only one who had them. She wasn't alone. She wasn't broken. Dr. Jessica Vera will spend the rest of her life sharing her story and solution with anyone needlessly suffering. So every morning they can wake up with peace, joy and happiness and be free from pain.

Dr. Jessica Vera, Best-Selling Author® of The Big Secret (contributing co-author with Jack Canfield), Amazon Best-selling author of Rise Up (Alma de Poder, in Spanish) and co-author of Fearless, has been featured on **CBS, Fox News, NBC, Bravo, A&E** and **TLN**, as she has built a real-life platform from her personal journey through trauma and has dedicated her life to learning all there is to know about psychological applied human sciences, trauma and the effect on human potential. In her early twenties, she founded three multi-million dollar corporations, was recognized as a Latin Female Entrepreneur of the Year; and became passionate about healing, learning and how to equip others to experience peace with their past and freedom to flourish in entrepreneurship. She is affectionately called a **Millionaire-Made Entrepreneur™** in the community, because she did not know the first thing about business when she started her career 30 years ago.

Dr. Jessica Vera today takes her social responsibility to be a voice for the voiceless through her flagship nonprofit Elite Foundation, Inc. EliteFundsFreedom.org is combating global human exploitation. This passion-purpose is shared by her Yayas, and her wonderful, selflessly supportive husband of 20 years and their two beautiful daughters.

 Wendy Elliott is an exceptional business entrepreneur with over two decades of experience in neuroscience healthcare management and executive corporate development. She holds multiple advanced degrees, including an MBA with a specialization in healthcare administration and a master's degree in speech language pathology and audiology.

Very early on Wendy developed a love for communication. Her dedicated life's work and passion for helping people communicate better and have their voices heard started in grade school as she helped a classmate communicate his wants and needs better because of his articulation deficit. This was the catalyst to her professional career as a direct care provider empowering those that could not communicate improve their abilities to be more independent. Her focus then was on those who could not speak or communicate well because of trauma, physical injury or disease processes. Now, she has taken this passion-purpose and by teaming up with others in collaboration, she helps those who have lost their inner voice, be heard and no longer live in secrecy. She believes that courage can be taught, and we have a social responsibility to ensure that all who need help have access to it. Today Wendy advocates a leader's need to accelerate performance in order to drive business execution through powerful communication. She delivers her unique service through one-on- one coaching and group dynamics. Through her consultative approach, backed by rigorous evaluation, she assists professionals to develop strategies to gain influence and credibility, build strong stakeholder relationships, and motivate their employees and teams to drive business strategies forward.

Wendy grew up in rural West Virginia and was raised by her grandparents who adopted her at an early age. Although she was one of a blended sibling kinship of 9, she was raised as an only child. After the traumatic untimely loss of her father (who died at age 49 from a heart attack) when Wendy was 7, her mother became a single parent determined to not be affected by her loss. From this point on, Wendy describes that she embarked upon her life's journey to achieve. She completed her high school education by age

16 and her first Master's degree by age 21. She lived to demonstrate to her mother that their sacrifices had paid off. Today a well-respected leader and influencer in her professional realm, her mother and father are undoubtedly smiling down at her daily and are proud of all she has accomplished and especially proud of how she tirelessly works to help others.

<u>ACKNOWLEDGMENTS</u>

Wendy and Jessica would like to extend their appreciation to a few people, who without them, this journey would have never been possible.

Raymond Meinhardt and Ariel Parma, the two exceptional men in our lives, respectively. Thank you for your support, willingness to do anything just to give us the space and time that we needed to accomplish this goal. It could have never been done without you!

To our respective families and Samantha and Miranda, you are all inspirations for us, we trust that through your love, we will continue to pave the way, for girls and women into the next century.

Jackie and Jim Moran thank you for your guidance, prayers, and encouragement.

Mr. Dennis Lauchner, we are most appreciative and blessed to embark on our collaborative passion-purpose to combat human exploitation with you by our side. Thank you very much for your compassionate heart, support, encouragement and your keen editorial skills.

Onward and upward ladies there is much to do in the world!

Reference List

Introduction

Lindenfeld, George L. Ph.D. Brain on Fire: A Therapist's Guide to Extinguishing the Flames of PTSD. CreateSpace Independent Publishing Platform, 2016.

Chapter One

19th Amendment. Amendment history

American Women in World War II: On the Home Front and Beyond. American women in WWII

Austen, Jane. **Pride and Prejudice**. New York: Modern Library, 1995. Print.

Glazebrook, Allison and Nicola Mellor. "Bodies and Sexuality." Cultural History of Women IN ANTIGUITY. Ed. Janet Tulloch. New York: Bloomsbury, 2013. 33-55. Print.

Hughes, Kathryn. Gender Roles in the 19th Century. gender roles in the 19th century.

Livesey, Chris, AS Sociology for AQA. 2nd ed. UK: Hodder Education, 2005. Web. 9, Oct. 2015.

Plante, Thomas Ph.D. Do the Right Thing.
https://www.psychologytoday.com/blog/do-the-right-thing

Tulloch, Janet H. A. Cultural History of Women IN ANTIGUITY. London: Bloomsbury, 2013. Print.

"The Role of Woman." Torah 101. Mechon Mamre, 24 Jan. 2012. Web, 01 Aug. 2015.

Williamson, Sally. The Hidden Factor: Executive Presence: How to Find It, Keep It and Leverage It. Atlanta, GA, Sally Williamson & Assoc., 2011.

Chapter Two

Casey E. Copen, Ph.D.; Kimberly Daniels, Ph.D.; Jonathan Vespa, Ph.D.; and William D. Mosher, Ph.D., First Marriages in the United States: Data From the 2006–2010 National Survey of Family Growth. National Health Statistics Report. Division of Vital Statistics. Number 49. March 22, 2012.

The Definition of Marriage. Merriam-Webster.

Chapter Three

Applebaum, Audet & Miller. "Gender and leadership? Leadership and gender? A journey through the landscape of theories." 2003, p. 44.
https://www.researchgate.net/publication/235285425_Gender_and_Leadership_
Leadership_and_Gender_A_Journey_Through_the_Landscape_of_Theories

Azar, Beth, "A New Stress Paradigm for Women." American Psychological Association. APA, July-Aug. 2000. Web 16 Mar 2017.

Bailey, Regina. "Do You Have Stellar Memory? It May Be Your Hippocampus." About Education. About.com 18 Dec. 2017. Web 17 Mar. 2017

Bavolek, Stephen. Male and Female Brain Functioning: Left Brain and Right Brain. Sacramento, CA: Birth and Beyond Program. Feb. 2012. PPT.

Billing, Yvonne and Alvesson, Mats. "Questioning the Notion of Feminine Leadership: A Critical Perspective on the Gender Labelling of Leadership." Volume 7, Issue 3. July 2000. Pages 144–157.

Boys and Girls" Brains Are Different: Gender Differences in Language Appear Biological." Science Daily. Northwestern University, 5 Mar. 2008.

Burman, Douglas D., Tali Bitan, and James R. Booth, "Sex Differences in Neural Processing of Language Among Children." Neuropscyhologia 46.5 (2008): 1349-1362. NCBI. U.S. Library of Medicine, 04 Jan. 2008. Web Mar. 2017

"The Bottom Line: Corporate Performance and Women's Representation on Boards." 2007.
http://www.catalyst.org/knowledge/bottom-line-corporate-performance-and-womens-representation-boards

"Cardoso, Christopher, et al. "Stress-induced Negative Mood Moderates the Relation between Oxytocin Administration and Trust: Evidence for the Tend-and-befriend Response to Stress?" Psychological Review 107.3 (2000): 411-29. Scholars at Harvard. Harvard Web Publishing. Web 16 Mar. 2017

Christman & McClelland "Executive Leadership for Women." 2008. P. 20. http://files.eric.ed.gov/fulltext/ED504434.pdf

Collignon, O., S. et al., "Women Process Multisensory Emotion Expressions More Efficiently than Man." Neuropsychology 48.1 (2010): 220-25. Science Direct. Elsevier. Web 17 Mar 2017

Duffy, J. A., Fox, S., Punnett, B. J., & Gregory, A. (2006). Successful women of the Americas: The same or different? [Electronic version] Management Research News, 29(9), 552-572. from Emerald.

Eagly, A. H., & Carli, L. L. (2007). Women and the labyrinth of leadership [Electronic version]. Harvard Business Review, 63-71. from EBSCOhost.

Ferris, Timothy. The 4-Hour Workweek. New Harvest, 2012. Print.

Grant, Bob. "Male and Female Brains Wired Differently." The Scientist. LabX Media Group, 04 Dec. 2013. Web 17 Mar. 2017

Gurian, Michael, and Barbara Annis. Leadership and the Sexes: Using Gender Science to Create Success in Business. San Francisco: Jossey-Bass, 2008. Print.

Hatcher, C. (2000). Refashioning a passionate manager: Gender at work [Electronic version]. Gender, Work and Organization, 10(4), 391-412. from Proquest.

Investopedia. "What is a 'Venture Capitalist'."

http://www.investopedia.com/terms/a/angelinvestor.asp#ixz z4bhDkK57x

Ingalhalikar, M., et. al. "Sex Differences in the Structural Connectome of the Human Brain." Proceeding of the National Academy of Sciences 111.2 (2013): 823-28. PNAS. Proceedings of National Academy of Science of the U.S., 01 Nov. 2013, Web 17 Mar. 2017

"It's Partly in Your Mind." WSJ. 11 Apr. 2011. Web 20 Aug, 2015.

Jacobs, D. (2007). Powerplay: Women, leadership and the getting of power [Electronic version]. Ivey Business Journal Online, Sept/Oct from Proquest.

Kaputa, Catherine. The Female Brand: Using the Female Mindset to Succeed in Business. Nicholas Brealey Publishing. 2009.

Kinsley, Craig and Lambert, Kelly. "The Maternal Brain." Scientific American. Nature America, Inc., Jan. 2006. Web 16 Mar. 2017.

McCarthy, Lauren. "Evolutionary and Biochemical Explanation for a Unique Female Stress Response: Tend-and-befriend. SAPA Project Test. Rochester Institute of Technology. Feb. 2005. Web 16 Mar. 2017.

"Men and Women Shown to Hear Differently." Medscape News & Perspective. WebMD LLC, 30 Nov 2000. Feb 2017

Moore, Caitlin S., et al. "Gender Differences in Neuropsychological Performance in Individuals with Atherosclerosis: Impact of Vascular Function." Journal of Clinical and Experiential Neuropsychology 33.1 (2011): 9-16. NCBI. U.S. National Library of Medicine, 28 May 2015.

Oakley, J. G. (2000). Gender-based barriers to senior management positions: Understanding the scarcity of female CEOs [Electronic version]. Journal of Business Ethics, 27, 321-334. from SpringerLink.

Olsson, S. (2000). Acknowledging the female archetype: Women managers' narratives of gender [Electronic version]. Women in Management Review, 15(5/6), 296-303. from Proquest.

Regine, B., & Lewin, R. (2003). Third possibility: The invisible edge that women have in complex organizations [Electronic version]. The Learning Organization, 10(6), 347- 352. from Emerald.

Shaywitz, B. A., et al. "Sex Differences in Functional Organization of the Brain for Language." Nature 373.6515 (1995): 607-09. NCBI. U.S. National Library of Medicine.

Shontell, Alyson. "Let's Be Real About The Lack Of Women In Tech." October 2010.
http://www.businessinsider.com/lets-be-real-about-the-lack-of-women-in-tech-2010-10

Stelter, N. Z. (2008). Gender differences in leadership: Current social issues and future organizational implications [Electronic version]. The Journal of Leadership Studies, 8(4), 88-99. from Proquest.

Stoet, Gijsbert, et al. "Are Women Better than Men at Multitasking?" BMC Psychology. BioMed Central Ltd. 24 Oct. 2013. Web 16 Mar. 2017.

Taylor, Shelley E., et al. "Biobehavioral Responses to Stress in Females-Tend-and-befriend. Not Fight-or-flight." Psychological Review 107.3 (2000): 411-29. Scholars at Harvard. Harvard Web Publishing. Web 17 Mar. 2017

Weyer, B. (2007). Twenty years later: Explaining the persistence of the glass ceiling for women leaders [Electronic version]. Women in Management Review, 22(6), 482-496. from Emerald.

Witelson, S.F.I.J. Glezer, and D. L. Kigar. "Women Have Greater Density of Neurons in Posterior Temporal Cortex." Journal of Neuroscience, 15.5 (1995): 3418-3428. Society for Neuroscience.

Wood, J.L, et al. "Morphology of the Ventral Frontal Cortex: Relationship of Femininity and Social Cognition." Cerebral Cortex 18.3 (2007):534-40. Oxford Journal. Oxford University Press, 14 June 2007. Web 17 Mar. 2017

Zaidi, Zeenar F. "Gender Differences in Human Brain: A Review." The Open Anatomy Journey (2010): 37-55. Betham Open. 14 Apr. 2010. Web 18 Mar. 2017.

Chapter Four

Akbari, Mohamad, et al. "Stress Coping Skills Training and Distress in Women with Breast Cancer." Procedia - Social and Behavioral Sciences, Volume 159, 23. December 2014.

Bruno, U.D.O. & Njoku, Joyce. "The role of the teacher in improving students self-esteem." Scholarly Journal of Education Vol. 3(6), pp. 58-61, September 2014.

Csikszentmihalyi, Mihaly. Flow: The Psychology of Optimal Experience. New York: Harper & Row, 1990.

Dee, J., Henkin, A., and Duemer, L. (2003) "Structural antecedents and psychological correlates of teacher empowerment", Journal of Educational Administration, Vol. 41 Issue: 3, pp.257-277.

Dove Self-Esteem Project. http://selfesteem.dove.us/

First author, Lin Bian, describes the research. This material relates to a paper that appeared in the Jan. 27 2017, issue of Science, published by AAAS. The paper, by L. Bian at University of Illinois at Urbana-Champaign in Champaign, IL, and colleagues was titled, "Gender stereotypes about intellectual ability emerge early and influence children's interests."

Garrety, K., Badham, R., Morrigan, V., Rifkin, W., and Zanko, M. (2003) The use of personality typing in organizational change: Discourse, emotions, and the reflexive subject. Human Relations, 56 (2), 211-235.

Girls Inc. "The Supergirl Dilemma: Girls Feel the Pressure to Be Perfect, Accomplished, Thin, and Accommodating." PR Newswire Association LLC. 2006.

Hinshaw, S. and Kranz, R. "The Triple Bind: Saving Our Teenage Girls From Today's Pressures and Conflicting Exploitations." December 2009.

John T. Cacioppo Wendi L. Gardner Gary G. Berntson, Beyond Bipolar Conceptualizations and Measures: The Case of Attitudes and Evaluative Space, First Published January 1, 1997, Web 23 Mar 2017.

Kelly MM, Tyrka AR, Anderson GM, Price LH, Carpenter LL. "Sex differences in emotional and physiological responses to the Trier Social Stress Test." J Behav Ther Exp Psychiatry. 2008 Mar;39(1):87-98. Epub 2007 Mar 12.

Laschinger, H., Finegan, J., Shamian, J., and Wilk, P. (2004) "A longitudinal analysis of the impact of workplace empowerment on work satisfaction." Volume 25, Issue 4. June 2004. Pages 527–545.

Murray CJ, Lopez AD. "Global mortality, disability, and the contribution of risk factors: Global Burden of Disease Study." Lancet. 1997.

Rick Hanson, Ph.D. Psychologist; Author, 'Hardwiring Happiness.' Article

"Confronting Negativity Bias." Huffington Post, Web 21 Mar 2017.

Safura et al. "The Self-Esteem: A Review Literature." International Journal of   African and Asian Studies. Vol. 9, 2015.

Seminowicz DA, Mayberg HS, McIntosh AR, Goldapple K, Kennedy S,   Segal Z, Rafi-Tari S. (2004) Limbic-frontal circuitry in major depression: a path modeling metanalysis.

Chapter Five

Angst J, Dobler-Mikola A. Do the diagnostic criteria determine the sex ratio in depression? J Affect Disord. 1984;7:189–198. doi: 10.1016/0165-0327(84)90040-5. [PubMed] [Cross Ref]

Arnold AP, Breedlove SM. Organizational and activational effects of sex steroids on brain and behavior: a reanalysis. Horm Behav. 1985;19:469–498.   doi: 10.1016/0018-506X(85)90042-X. [PubMed][Cross Ref]

Arnold AP, Chen X, Itoh Y. What a difference an X or Y makes: sex chromosomes, gene dose, and epigenetics in sexual differentiation. Handb Exp Pharmacol. 2012;259:2–9. [PMC free article] [PubMed]

Arnold AP. The organizational-activational hypothesis as the foundation for a unified theory of sexual differentiation of all mammalian tissues. Horm Behav. 2009;55:570–578. doi: 10.1016/j.yhbeh.2009.03.011. [PMC free article] [PubMed] [Cross Ref]

Baum MJ. Differentiation of coital behavior in mammals: a comparative analysis. Neurosci Biobehav Rev. 1979;3:265–284. doi: 10.1016/0149-7634(79)90013-7. [PubMed] [Cross Ref]

Belmaker RH, Agam G. Major depressive disorder. N Engl J Med. 2008;358:55–68. doi: 10.1056/NEJMra073096. [PubMed] [Cross Ref]

Berger M, Bossert S, Krieg JC, Dirlich G, Ettmeier W, Schreiber W, von Zerssen D. Interindividual differences in the susceptibility of the cortisol system: an important factor for the degree of hypercortisolism in stress situations? Biol Psychiatry. 1987;22:1327–1339. doi: 10.1016/0006-3223(87)90067-9. [PubMed] [Cross Ref]

Boatman, Jazmine Ph.D. et al. "Women as Mentors: Does She or Doesn't She? A Global Study of Businesswomen and Mentoring." 2011.

Bogner HR, Gallo JJ. Are higher rates of depression in women accounted for by differential symptom reporting? Soc Psychiatry Psychiatr Epidemiol. 2004;39:126–132. doi: 10.1007/s00127-004-0714-z.[PMC free article] [PubMed] [Cross Ref]

Budefeld T, Grgurevic N, Tobet SA, Majdic G. Sex differences in brain developing in the presence or absence of gonads. Dev Neurobiol. 2008;68:981–995. doi: 10.1002/dneu.20638. [PMC free article][PubMed] [Cross Ref]

Chourbaji S, Pfeiffer N, Dormann C, Brandwein C, Fradley R, Sheardown M, Gass P. The suitability of 129SvEv mice for studying depressive-like behaviour: both males and females develop learned helplessness. Behav Brain Res. 2010;211:105–110. doi: 10.1016/j.bbr.2010.03.019. [PubMed] [Cross Ref]

(Chrisler, Joan and McCreary, Donald. "Handbook of Gender Research in Psychology." 2010.

Claustrat B, Chazot G, Brun J, Jordan D, Sassolas G. A chronobiological study of melatonin and cortisol secretion in depressed subjects: plasma melatonin, a biochemical marker in major depression. Biol Psychiatry. 1984;19:1215–1228. [PubMed]

Craig AD. How do you feel–now? The anterior insula and human awareness. Nat Rev Neurosci. 2009;10:59–70. doi: 10.1038/nrn2555. [PubMed] [Cross Ref]

Dalla C, Edgecomb C, Whetstone AS, Shors TJ. Females do not express learned helplessness like males do. Neuropsychopharmacology. 2008;33:1559–1569. doi: 10.1038/sj.npp.1301533. [PubMed][Cross Ref]

Deuschle M, Schweiger U, Weber B, Gotthardt U, Korner A, Schmider J, Standhardt H, Lammers CH, Heuser I. Diurnal activity and pulsatility of the hypothalamus-pituitary-adrenal system in male depressed patients and healthy controls. J Clin Endocrinol Metab. 1997;82:234–238. doi: 10.1210/jcem.82.1.3689.[PubMed] [Cross Ref]

Drevets WC, Ongur D, Price JL. Reduced glucose metabolism in the subgenual prefrontal cortex in unipolar depression. Mol Psychiatry. 1998;3:190–191. doi: 10.1038/sj.mp.4000380. [PubMed] [Cross Ref]

Drevets WC, Savitz J, Trimble M. The subgenual anterior cingulate cortex in mood disorders. CNS Spectr. 2008;13:663–681. [PMC free article] [PubMed]

Ducottet C, Aubert A, Belzung C. Susceptibility to subchronic unpredictable stress is related to individual reactivity to threat stimuli in mice. Behav Brain Res. 2004;155:291–299. doi: 10.1016/j.bbr.2004.04.020. [PubMed] [Cross Ref]

Engel K, Bandelow B, Gruber O, Wedekind D. Neuroimaging in anxiety disorders. J Neural Transm. 2009;116:703–716. doi: 10.1007/s00702-008-0077-9. [PMC free article] [PubMed] [Cross Ref]

Entsuah AR, Huang H, Thase ME. Response and remission rates in different subpopulations with major depressive disorder administered venlafaxine, selective serotonin reuptake inhibitors, or placebo. J Clin Psychiatry. 2001;62:869–877. doi: 10.4088/JCP.v62n1106. [PubMed] [Cross Ref]

Farber, Neil: https://www.psychologytoday.com/blog/the-blame-game/201609/the-truth-about-the-law-attraction)

Ferketich AK, Schwartzbaum JA, Frid DJ, Moeschberger ML. Depression as an antecedent to heart disease among women and men in the NHANES I study. National health and nutrition examination survey. Arch Intern Med. 2000;160:1261–1268. doi: 10.1001/archinte.160.9.1261. [PubMed] [Cross Ref]

Frank E, Carpenter LL, Kupfer DJ. Sex differences in recurrent depression: are there any that are significant? Am J Psychiatry. 1988;145:41–45. doi: 10.1176/ajp.145.1.41. [PubMed] [Cross Ref]

Gaiteri C, Guilloux JP, Lewis DA, Sibille E. Altered gene synchrony suggests a combined hormone-mediated dysregulated state in major depression. PLoS One. 2010;5:e9970. doi: 10.1371/journal.pone.0009970. [PMC free article] [PubMed] [Cross Ref]

Groenink L, Dirks A, Verdouw PM, Schipholt M, Veening JG, van der Gugten J, Olivier B. HPA axis dysregulation in mice overexpressing corticotropin releasing hormone. Biol Psychiatry. 2002;51:875–881. doi: 10.1016/S0006-3223(02)01334-3. [PubMed] [Cross Ref]

Hamilton JA, Grant M, Jensvold MF. Sex and treatment of depression: When does it matter? In: Jensvold MF, Halbreich U, Hamilton JA, editors. Psychopharmacology and Women: Sex, Gender, and Hormones. Washington, DC: American Psychiatric Press; 1996. pp. 241–257.

Hill, Napoleon. Think and Grow Rich. New York: Fawcett Books, 1987. Print.

Jacobs PA, Strong JA. A case of human intersexuality having a possible XXY sex-determining mechanism. Nature. 1959;183:302–303. doi: 10.1038/183302a0. [PubMed] [Cross Ref]

Kelly MM, Tyrka AR, Anderson GM, Price LH, Carpenter LL. Sex differences in emotional and physiological responses to the trier social stress test. J Behav Ther Exp Psychiatry. 2008;39:87–98.

doi: 10.1016/j.jbtep.2007.02.003. [PMC free article] [PubMed] [Cross Ref]

Kendler KS, Prescott CA, Myers J, Neale MC. The structure of genetic and environmental risk factors for common psychiatric and substance use disorders in men and women. Arch Gen Psychiatry. 2003;60:929–937. doi: 10.1001/archpsyc.60.9.929. [PubMed] [Cross Ref]

Kessler RC, Berglund P, Demler O, Jin R, Merikangas KR, Walters EE. Lifetime prevalence and age-of-onset distributions of DSM-IV disorders in the national comorbidity survey replication. Arch Gen Psychiatry. 2005;62:593–602. doi: 10.1001/archpsyc.62.6.593. [PubMed] [Cross Ref]

Knol MJ, Twisk JW, Beekman AT, Heine RJ, Snoek FJ, Pouwer F. Depression as a risk factor for the onset of type 2 diabetes mellitus. A meta-analysis. Diabetologia. 2006;49:837–845. doi: 10.1007/s00125-006-0159-x. [PubMed] [Cross Ref]

Koopman P, Gubbay J, Vivian N, Goodfellow P, Lovell-Badge R. Male development of chromosomally female mice transgenic for Sry. Nature. 1991;351:117–121. doi: 10.1038/351117a0. [PubMed] [Cross Ref]

Kornstein SG, Schatzberg AF, Thase ME, Yonkers KA, McCullough JP, Keitner GI, Gelenberg AJ, Ryan CE, Hess AL, Harrison W, Davis SM, Keller MB. Gender differences in chronic major and double depression. J Affect Disord. 2000;60:1–11. doi: 10.1016/S0165-0327(99)00158-5. [PubMed] [Cross Ref]

Krishnan V, Han MH, Graham DL, Berton O, Renthal W, Russo SJ, Laplant Q, Graham A, Lutter M, Lagace DC, Ghose S, Reister R, Tannous P, Green TA, Neve RL, Chakravarty S, Kumar A, Eisch AJ, Self DW, Lee FS, Tamminga CA, Cooper DC, Gershenfeld HK,

Nestler EJ. Molecular adaptations underlying susceptibility and resistance to social defeat in brain reward regions. Cell. 2007;131:391–404. doi: 10.1016/j.cell.2007.09.018. [PubMed] [Cross Ref]

Lechter, Sharon. http://sharonlechter.com/

Maggie Baker. http://www.maggiebakerphd.com/

Mann JJ. Neurobiology of suicidal behaviour. Nat Rev Neurosci. 2003;4:819–828. doi: 10.1038/nrn1220. [PubMed] [Cross Ref]

Martin EI, Ressler KJ, Binder E, Nemeroff CB. The neurobiology of anxiety disorders: brain imaging, genetics, and psychoneuroendocrinology. Clin Lab Med. 2010;30:865–891. doi: 10.1016/j.cll.2010.07.006.[PubMed] [Cross Ref]

Mayberg HS, Brannan SK, Tekell JL, Silva JA, Mahurin RK, McGinnis S, Jerabek PA. Regional metabolic effects of fluoxetine in major depression: serial changes and relationship to clinical response. Biol Psychiatry. 2000;48:830–843. doi: 10.1016/S0006-3223(00)01036-2. [PubMed] [Cross Ref]

Mayberg HS, Lozano AM, Voon V, McNeely HE, Seminowicz D, Hamani C, Schwalb JM, Kennedy SH. Deep brain stimulation for treatment-resistant depression. Neuron. 2005;45:651–660. doi: 10.1016/j.neuron.2005.02.014. [PubMed] [Cross Ref]

Mayberg HS. Limbic-cortical dysregulation: a proposed model of depression. J Neuropsychiatry Clin Neurosci. 1997;9:471–481. doi: 10.1176/jnp.9.3.471. [PubMed] [Cross Ref]

McCarthy MM, Arnold AP. Reframing sexual differentiation of the brain. Nat Neurosci. 2011;14:677–683. doi: 10.1038/nn.2834. [PMC free article] [PubMed] [Cross Ref]

McCarthy MM, Wright CL, Schwarz JM. New tricks by an old dogma: mechanisms of the organizational/activational hypothesis of steroid-mediated sexual differentiation of brain and behavior. Horm Behav. 2009;55:655–665. doi: 10.1016/j.yhbeh.2009.02.012. [PMC free article] [PubMed][Cross Ref]

Michelson D, Stratakis C, Hill L, Reynolds J, Galliven E, Chrousos G, Gold P. Bone mineral density in women with depression. N Engl J Med. 1996;335:176–1181. doi: 10.1056/NEJM199610173351602.[PubMed] [Cross Ref]

Monk CS, Klein RG, Telzer EH, Schroth EA, Mannuzza S, Moulton JL, 3rd, Guardino M, Masten CL, McClure-Tone EB, Fromm S, Blair RJ, Pine DS, Ernst M. Amygdala and nucleus accumbens activation to emotional facial expressions in children and adolescents at risk for major depression. Am J Psychiatry. 2008;165:90–98. doi: 10.1176/appi.ajp.2007.06111917. [PubMed] [Cross Ref]

Murray CJ, Lopez AD. Global mortality, disability, and the contribution of risk factors: global burden of disease study. Lancet. 1997;349:1436–1442. doi: 10.1016/S0140-6736(96)07495-8. [PubMed] [Cross Ref]

Muscat R, Willner P. Suppression of sucrose drinking by chronic mild unpredictable stress: a methodological analysis. Neurosci Biobehav Rev. 1992;16:507–517. doi: 10.1016/S0149-7634(05)80192-7. [PubMed] [Cross Ref]

Musselman DL, Evans DL, Nemeroff CB. The relationship of depression to cardiovascular disease: epidemiology, biology, and treatment. Arch Gen Psychiatry. 1998;55:580–592. doi: 10.1001/archpsyc.55.7.580. [PubMed] [Cross Ref]

Najt P, Fusar-Poli P, Brambilla P. Co-occurring mental and substance abuse disorders: a review on the potential predictors and clinical outcomes. Psychiatry Res. 2011;186:159–164. doi: 10.1016/j.psychres.2010.07.042. [PubMed] [Cross Ref]

O'Brien JT, Lloyd A, McKeith I, Gholkar A, Ferrier N. A longitudinal study of hippocampal volume, cortisol levels, and cognition in older depressed subjects. Am J Psychiatry. 2004;161:2081–2090. doi: 10.1176/appi.ajp.161.11.2081. [PubMed] [Cross Ref]

Papp M, Willner P, Muscat R. An animal model of anhedonia: attenuation of sucrose consumption and place preference conditioning by chronic unpredictable mild stress. Psychopharmacology (Berl) 1991;104:255–259. doi: 10.1007/BF02244188. [PubMed] [Cross Ref]

Parker KL, Schimmer BP. Steroidogenic factor 1: a key determinant of endocrine development and function. Endocr Rev. 1997;18:361–377. doi: 10.1210/edrv.18.3.0301. [PubMed] [Cross Ref]

Pezawas L, Meyer-Lindenberg A, Drabant EM, Verchinski BA, Munoz KE, Kolachana BS, Egan MF, Mattay VS, Hariri AR, Weinberger DR. 5-HTTLPR polymorphism impacts human cingulate-amygdala interactions: a genetic susceptibility mechanism for depression. Nat Neurosci. 2005;8:828–834. doi: 10.1038/nn1463. [PubMed] [Cross Ref]

Pothion S, Bizot JC, Trovero F, Belzung C. Strain differences in sucrose preference and in the consequences of unpredictable chronic mild stress. Behav Brain Res. 2004;155:135–146. doi: 10.1016/j.bbr.2004.04.008. [PubMed] [Cross Ref]

Quitkin FM, Stewart JW, McGrath PJ, Taylor BP, Tisminetzky MS, Petkova E, Chen Y, Ma G, Klein DF. Are there differences between women's and men's antidepressant responses? Am J Psychiatry. 2002;159:1848–1854. doi: 10.1176/appi.ajp.159.11.1848. [PubMed] [Cross Ref]

Sachar EJ, Hellman L, Roffwarg HP, Halpern FS, Fukushima DK, Gallagher TF. Disrupted 24-hour patterns of cortisol secretion in psychotic depression. Arch Gen Psychiatry. 1973;28:19–24. doi: 10.1001/archpsyc.1973.01750310011002. [PubMed] [Cross Ref]

Schulz KM, Molenda-Figueira HA, Sisk CL. Back to the future: the organizational-activational hypothesis adapted to puberty and adolescence. Horm Behav. 2009;55:597–604. doi: 10.1016/j.yhbeh.2009.03.010. [PMC free article] [PubMed] [Cross Ref]

Schulz R, Beach SR, Ives DG, Martire LM, Ariyo AA, Kop WJ. Association between depression and mortality in older adults: the cardiovascular health study. Arch Intern Med. 2000;160:1761–1768. doi: 10.1001/archinte.160.12.1761. [PubMed] [Cross Ref]

Seminowicz DA, Mayberg HS, McIntosh AR, Goldapple K, Kennedy S, Segal Z, Rafi-Tari S. Limbic-frontal circuitry in major depression: a path modeling metanalysis. Neuroimage. 2004;22:409–418. doi: 10.1016/j.neuroimage.2004.01.015. [PubMed] [Cross Ref]

Sheline YI, Barch DM, Donnelly JM, Ollinger JM, Snyder AZ, Mintun MA. Increased amygdala response to masked emotional faces in depressed subjects resolves with antidepressant treatment: an fMRI study. Biol Psychiatry. 2001;50:651–658. doi: 10.1016/S0006-3223(01)01263-X. [PubMed] [Cross Ref]

Siegle GJ, Steinhauer SR, Thase ME, Stenger VA, Carter CS. Can't shake that feeling: event-related fMRI assessment of sustained amygdala activity in response to emotional information in depressed individuals. Biol Psychiatry. 2002;51:693–707. doi: 10.1016/S0006-3223(02)01314-8. [PubMed][Cross Ref]

Siegle GJ, Thompson W, Carter CS, Steinhauer SR, Thase ME. Increased amygdala and decreased dorsolateral prefrontal BOLD responses in unipolar depression: related and independent features. Biol Psychiatry. 2007;61:198–209. doi: 10.1016/j.biopsych.2006.05.048. [PubMed] [Cross Ref]

Silverstein B. Gender difference in the prevalence of clinical depression: the role played by depression associated with somatic symptoms. Am J Psychiatry. 1999;156:480–482. [PubMed]

Sinclair AH, Berta P, Palmer MS, Hawkins JR, Griffiths BL, Smith MJ, Foster JW, Frischauf AM, Lovell-Badge R, Goodfellow PN. A gene from the human sex-determining region encodes a protein with homology to a conserved DNA-binding motif. Nature. 1990;346:240–244. doi: 10.1038/346240a0.[PubMed] [Cross Ref]

Surget A, Wang Y, Leman S, Ibarguen-Vargas Y, Edgar N, Griebel G, Belzung C, Sibille E. Corticolimbic transcriptome changes are state-dependent and region-specific in a rodent model of depression and of antidepressant reversal. Neuropsychopharmacology. 2009;34:1363–1380. doi: 10.1038/npp.2008.76. [PMC free article] [PubMed] [Cross Ref]

Townsend JD, Eberhart NK, Bookheimer SY, Eisenberger NI, Foland-Ross LC, Cook IA, Sugar CA, Altshuler LL. fMRI activation in the amygdala and the orbitofrontal cortex in unmedicated subjects with major depressive disorder. Psychiatry Res. 2010;183:209–217. doi: 10.1016/j.pscychresns.2010.06.001.[PMC free article] [PubMed] [Cross Ref]

Trainor BC, Takahashi EY, Campi KL, Florez SA, Greenberg GD, Laman-Maharg A, Laredo SA, Orr VN, Silva AL, Steinman MQ. Sex differences in stress-induced social withdrawal: independence from adult gonadal hormones and inhibition of female phenotype by corncob bedding. Horm Behav. 2013;63:543–550. doi: 10.1016/j.yhbeh.2013.01.011. [PMC free article] [PubMed] [Cross Ref]

Tsankova NM, Berton O, Renthal W, Kumar A, Neve RL, Nestler EJ. Sustained hippocampal chromatin regulation in a mouse model of depression and antidepressant action. Nat Neurosci. 2006;9:519–525. doi: 10.1038/nn1659. [PubMed] [Cross Ref]

Vogt BA. Pain and emotion interactions in subregions of the cingulate gyrus. Nat Rev Neurosci. 2005;6:533–544. doi: 10.1038/nrn1704. [PMC free article] [PubMed] [Cross Ref]

Weissman MM, Klerman GL. Sex-differences and epidemiology of depression. Arch Gen Psychiatry. 1977;34:98–111. doi: 10.1001/archpsyc.1977.01770130100011. [PubMed] [Cross Ref]

WHO . World Health Organization - The Global Burden of Disease - 2004 Update. Geneva, Switzerland: WHO Library; 2004. p. 2008.

Willner P. Validation criteria for animal models of human mental disorders: learned helplessness as a paradigm case. Prog Neuropsychopharmacol Biol Psychiatry. 1986;10:677–690. doi: 10.1016/0278-5846(86)90051-5. [PubMed] [Cross Ref]

Young MA, Fogg LF, Scheftner WA, Keller MB, Fawcett JA. Sex differences in the lifetime prevalence of depression: does varying the diagnostic criteria reduce the female/male ratio? J Affect Disord. 1990;18:187–192. doi: 10.1016/0165-0327(90)90035-7. [PubMed] [Cross Ref]

Chapter 6

Augustine, Ann. "How Collaboration Can Work for Business." October 2016.
https://www.lifewire.com/how-collaboration-can-work-for-business-771565

Finn, Heather. "7 Famous People Who Took Big Career Risks and Never Looked Back." Levo League, LLC. January 04, 2016.
https://www.levo.com/posts/7-famous-people-who-took-big-career-risks-and-never-looked-back

Rosen, Evan. "Smashing Silos." Bloomberg Businessweek. February 2010.
https://www.bloomberg.com/news/articles/2010-02-05/smashing-silos

Chapter 7

Cordora, Dame DC. Money & You: Access to Cash. Waterfront Press, 2016

Daskal, Lolly. "7 Powerful Ways to Turn Every Failure Into Success." September 2016.

http://www.inc.com/lolly-daskal/7-surprising-ways-to-turn-every-failure-into-success.html

Fakaro, Nikos. "The Lone Nut + The Follower = A Movement." 2012. Video.

https://www.youtube.com/watch?v=256eKjULdgQ

Fallon, Nicole. "5 Questions To Ask Before Choosing A Mentor." October 2014.

http://www.huffingtonpost.com/2014/10/21/finding-a-mentor-questions_n_6020816.html

Han, Lei. "Soft Skills-Ask a Wharton MBA" Soft skills Membership, n.d.

https://bemycareercoach.com/soft-skills/list-soft-skills.html Accessed 23, Mar. 2017

Herzlinger, Regina. "Why Innovation in Health Care Is So Hard." May 2006.

https://hbr.org/2006/05/why-innovation-in-health-care-is-so-hard

Kalman, Frank. "Top 10 Leadership Soft Skills". Chief Learning Officer. December 17, 2012.

http://www.clomedia.com/2012/12/17/top-10-leadership-soft-skills/. Accessed 23, Mar. 2017.

Legally Blonde (Comedy) (2001) 2004 by Raymond Weschler

http://www.eslnotes.com/movies/pdf/Legally-Blonde.pdf

Leanne. "What is mentorship, and why should you care?" February 2016.

http://www.leannewsmith.com/what-is-mentorship-and-why-should-you-care/

Louisehay.com, Heal your body; books and health @Hayhouse; publication 1/1/84

Maxwell, John, 21 irrefutable laws of leadership, 10th Anniversary Edition, United States of America, Thomas Nelson 2007; ch 1 pp1-11.

Marcel M. Robles, Executive Perceptions of the Top 10 Soft Skills Needed in Today's Workplace, Business Communication Quarterly, 75(4) 453–465 (pdf)

Marie. "The Wisdom of Elle Woods." December 2012.

http://survivelaw.com/index.php/blogs/procrastination/1081-the-wisdom-of-elle-woods

Marshall, Lisa. "How to Fix a Bad First Impression" May 2015.

http://www.quickanddirtytips.com/business-career/communication/how-to-fix-a-bad-first-impression?page=2

McKeown, Greg. "The Unimportance of Practically Everything." Harvard Business Review, Harvard Business School Publishing, 23 July 2014, hbr.org/2012/05/the-unimportance-of-practical. Accessed 22 Mar. 2017

Mind Tools. "What is Leadership?" Mind Tools Ltd, 1996-2017.

https://www.mindtools.com/pages/article/newLDR_41.htm

Soft Skills. https://en.wikipedia.org/wiki/Soft_skills

Parr, Sam. "Getting Called "Sweetie" helped this entrepreneur Create a $100M Business", theHustle, March 13, 2017, https://thehustle.co/hint-is-100m-business. Accessed March 23, 2017

Rast, Heather. "7 Ways To Build Trust With Your Clients." http://soloprpro.com/7-ways-to-build-trust-with-your-clients/

Rouse, Margaret, and Ivy Wigmore. "96-Minute Rule." WhatIs.com, SearchCRM.com, Aug. 2013, whatis.techtarget.com/definition/96-minute-rule.

Sexton, Marie. http://www.goodreads.com/author/quotes/3292500.Marie_Sexton

Smith, Jacquelyn. "6 Tips For Dealing With People Who Doubt Your Ability To Succeed." August 2014. http://www.businessinsider.com/when-people-doubt-your-ability-to-succeed-2014-8

Starr, Karla. "The Science of First Impressions." February 2013. https://www.psychologytoday.com/blog/the-science-luck/201302/the-science-first-impressions

Tracy, Brian. "How to Use The 80/20 Rule For Goal Setting." Brian Tracy's Self Improvement & Professional Development Blog, Brian Tracy International, 14 Mar. 2017, www.briantracy.com/blog/personal-success/how-to-use-the-80-20-rule-pareto-principle/. Accessed 22 Mar. 2017.

Walker, Jacqui. "Legally Blonde: The Elle Woods Guide to Law and Life." November 2015.

http://blog.legaler.com/2015/11/01/legally-blonde-the-elle-woods-guide-to-law-and-life/

Yamada, David. "Why so many managers are mediocre or bad: They weren't promoted because they were good leaders". Minding the WorkPlace: The New Workplace Institute Blog, July 27, 2011,

https://newworkplace.wordpress.com/2011/07/27/why-so-many-managers-are-mediocre-or-bad-they-werent-promoted-because-they-are-good-leaders/. Accessed March 23, 2017

Chapter 8

"47 Information Product Examples That Kick Ass." 2011-2017 Real Passive Income Ideas.

https://realpassiveincomeideas.com/information-product-examples/

Angeles, Sara. "Best Accounting Software for Small Business 2017." Business News Daily, Purch Group, Inc, 2 Nov. 2016,

www.businessnewsdaily.com/7543-best-accounting-software.html.%20Accessed%2022%20Mar.%202017.

Annis, B. and Gray, J. "Work With Me: The 8 Blind Spots Between Men and Women in Business." New York: Barbara Annis and John Gray, 2013.

Blitz, Matt. "The True Story of 'Hidden Figures' and the Women Who Crunched the Numbers for NASA." February 2017. http://www.popularmechanics.com/space/rockets/a24429/hidden-figures-real-story-nasa-women-computers/

Brem, Marion Luna. Women Make the Best Salesmen: Isn't It Time You Started Using Their Secrets? New York, Currency Doubleday, 2005.

Broder, Lindsay. "How to Develop the Soft Skills of the Successful Entrepreneur." February 2015.
https://www.entrepreneur.com/article/243059

"Facts Vs. Emotions: When to Use Each Tactic to Make a Sale." Business.com, Purch, 22 Feb. 2017,
www.business.com/articles/facts-vs-emotions-when-to-use-each-tactic-to-make-a-sale/

Gschwandtner, Gerhard. "The Right Questions Can Close More Sales More Often." 1998 - 2017 Personal Selling Power, Inc.
http://www.sellingpower.com/content/article/index.php?a=8875/the-right-questions-can-close-more-sales-more-often&page=2

Gurian, Michael, and Barbara Annis. Leadership and the Sexes: Using Gender Science to Create Success in Business. Jossey-Bass, 2008.

Holleran, Scott. "Movie Review: Hidden Figures." December 2016.
http://newromanticist.com/2016/movie-review-hidden-figures/

Knight, Dan. "Personal Computer History: The First 25 Years." April 2014.
http://lowendmac.com/2014/personal-computer-history-the-first-25-years/

"Lead Nurturing." Marketo, Marketo, Inc.om,
www.marketo.com/lead-nurturing/.

Levesque, Ryan. "Ask: The Counterintuitive Online Formula to Discover Exactly What Your Customers Want to Buy...Create a Mass of Raving Fans...and Take Any Business to the Next Level." April 2015.
http://www.goodreads.com

"Top 7 Soft Skills Of Successful Entrepreneurs." January 2015.
Youngupstarts.com

Mallikarjunan, Sam. "Why Managers Should Go See Hidden Figures Twice." February 2017.
https://thinkgrowth.org/why-managers-should-go-see-hidden-figures-twice-61943a255ab0%23.n90z0go5f

Moncrief, William C, et al. "Examining Gender Differences in Field Sales Organizations." Journal of Business Research, vol. 49, no. 3, Feb. 2000, pp. 245–257. ResearchGate, doi:10.1016/s0148-2963(99)00019-3.

Mulholland, Ben. "The 14 Best Organization Apps For Your Work and Life."
Process Street, Goodwinds INC, 3 Apr. 2016,
www.process.st/best-organization-apps/.%20Accessed%2022%20Mar.%202017.

Restauri, Denise. "Women Taking Action: 10 Top Female Founded Tech Startups." November 2016.
https://www.forbes.com/sites/deniserestauri/2016/11/13/women-taking-action-10-top-female-founded-tech-startups/%237921b0a67c34

Relander, Brett. "25 Payment Tools for Small Businesses, Freelancers and Startups." Entrepreneur, Entrepreneur Media Inc, 19 July 2016,
www.entrepreneur.com/article/276818.%20Accessed%2022%20Mar.%202017

Rivard, Johanna. "A Complete Guide to Social Media-Based Lead Generation." Marketing Insider Group, Marketing Insider Group, 17 June 2016,

marketinginsidergroup.com/content-marketing/complete-guide-social-media-based-lead-generation-software-companies/. Accessed 22 Mar. 2017.

Rouse, Margaret, and Tim Ehrens. "Customer Releationship Managment." TechTarget, SearchCRM.com, Nov. 4ADAD, searchcrm.techtarget.com/definition/CR. Accessed 22 Mar. 2017.

Sarbah, LaKisha. "Real Pain Points and Challenges for Women Entrepreneurs." Medium, Medium Coorporation, 27 Oct. 2016, medium.com/@lakishasarbah/real-pain-points-and-challenges-for-women-entrepreneurs-146fe702d5ce#.bgud5yq2a. Accessed 22 Mar. 2017.

Weller, Nathan B. "The 15 Best Webinar Software Products From Around The Web." Elegant Themes, Elegant Themes, Inc, 17 Jan. 2015,
www.elegantthemes.com/blog/resources/the-15-best-webinar-software-products-from-around-the-web.%20Accessed%2022%20Mar.%202017.

"What Is Cloud Storage? - Definition from Techopedia." Techopedia.com, Janalta Interactive Inc,

www.techopedia.com/definition/26535/cloud-storage.%20Accessed%2022%20Mar.%202017.

"What Is Email Automation?" Bigcommerce, Bigcommerce, Inc., 7 Oct. 2014,

www.bigcommerce.com/ecommerce-answers/what-email-automation/. Accessed 22 Mar. 2017.

Wright, Travis. "29 Favorite Business Tech Tools of Entrepreneurs in 2015." Inc.com, Inc., 13 Aug. 2015,

www.inc.com/travis-wright/28-favorite-tech-tools-for-small-business-entrepreneurs-in-2015.html. Accessed 22 Mar. 2017.

Chapter 9

Haisha, Lisa. "The Three Biggest Fears Women Have." The Huffington Post, TheHuffingtonPost.com, 20 Jan. 2011, www.huffingtonpost.com/lisa-haisha/women-fears_b_809148.html. Accessed 22 Mar. 2017.